LORD OF ECONOMIC KINGDOM

SECRET KEYS FOR KINGDOM BUSINESSES AND KINGDOMPRENEURS

LONNA HARDIN

LONNA HARDIN ENTERPRISES

CONTENTS

2.

3.

4.

5.

6.

7.

8.

9.

10.

11.

My Worship Is For Real

I am a worshipper. Ever since I was five years old, I remember singing and wanting to be a star. I grew up in the church. At a young age, all I knew was singing, music, and songwriting. I wrote songs and I would teach them to our church choir. At five, I acted like I was a world-renowned writer and director. Hearing my Aunt Gloria recall these stories makes me laugh!

As I grew older, my passion for music and writing grew. Here's a secret. I could not sing as a child! My older sister sang like a bird and I always admired her. I wanted to be like her. She got all the attention. She is full of poise, calm, and is confident and self-assured.

Unlike my sister, I was spontaneous, spunky, and full of life. I was bold, daring, and loved adventure. We came from a gifted, musical family. We had a deep, rich history of singing and songwriting. My father was a preacher, singer, and musician. My Mother was a singer and songwriter. My grandfather was a singer and traveled with a quartet.

As a child, my mother also always wanted to sing. She was an amazing singer and vocalist from a small town in Michigan who lacked opportunity. Born in Eau Claire, my grandparents later moved to a town named Dowagiac. My Mother was our queen and hero.

As a young girl, I always heard stories about my Mother's talent of songwriting and dream of singing. Here is one told throughout our family about how extraordinary her talent was.

When my mother was in the 8th grade, Motown had a contest. She entered a song she wrote called, "Where Did My Love Go?" and Motown sent her a contract. She was too young to understand a contract or hire a lawyer and she never sent the contract back.

The song was later released with a different name, with one word changed in the title. People everywhere were singing, "Baby, baby, where did our love go" with one word changed, and the rest is history!

Later, when my Mother was 18, she ran away to Chicago. During this time, she wrote another song called "Runaway Love." As fate would have it, she met someone while riding on a Greyhound bus. As a gift, she *sang (or wrote)* her song to them, and later, it became a hit for the Temptations.

Over time, I learned this about myself:

- Church, singing, music, and songwriting is all I've known my entire life.
- I am a worshipper.
- Sometimes we don't realize the value of who we are.
- Recognize your value, who you are and what you have to offer the
- world to expand and maximize the Kingdom of God.

Singing was all I wanted to do as a little girl. I performed anywhere I could. I would ask my teachers if I could sing in front of the class. I exhausted them by continuing to ask to sing, and eventually, they would let me.

I would get up and perform. I thought I was Aretha Franklin or Whitney Houston! It became a norm and my personal signature. Looking back, I'm still not quite sure how I convinced people to let me perform.

Most times, my voice would tremble. Nervousness would creep up in my stomach. I would freeze up and think, "I didn't sound like this during practice." My private victories were not translating into public victories.

I practiced at home with my sister. She often called me "tone deaf." I laughed about it then, and still laugh about it now. We have that kind of love and humor in our family. It's very dry. As time went on, I became embarrassed. I felt I could never completely express myself in the beautiful way that I wanted to.

I grew up in church with a deep passion for God. Looking back, I'm not sure where it came from. There was always something different about me. I was not like other kids. I was even different from my sisters.

I wrote letters to Jesus. Even as a child, I praised my Mom and thanked God for her life. At age six, I remember going on a fast with my Mom. She was believing God for a new job.

Likewise, when I ran into the dilemma of having a passion to sing, but not being able to, I went to God because I could not hold a steady note. I choked in front of people. I started to pray about it. I asked the Lord to, "please let me sing." I sought God nonstop. Over time, I found myself singing and sounding so beautiful. I was so surprised! Truly God answers prayer.

Even though I experienced small victories, I still froze in front of people. It happened so many times that I went to God again. "Lord, can you help me sing in front of people?" Before I knew it, I found myself standing in front of crowds singing with confidence. As a result, prayer became a lifestyle.

As a little girl, I prayed. In my teens, I veered off, but always returned to God in prayer. As a young adult, prayer led me to God every time. In the process, I transformed from singer to worshipper, and I became a lover of God.

The Lord wooed me. His awesome presence provoked me. He drew me with love and compassion so many times. I talked to Him about everything.

My intimate times of prayer and fasting were the best times of my life. When I look back, The Lord is front and center of what makes me most happy. He has defended me so many times. He has picked me up again and again. When my heart was broken, He was there to whisper, "I am here." Surely, He is the great I Am!

I love people too. I have always been very outgoing. Often, others did not perceive the depth of my love for God. Some said I was stuck up. Some called me "churchy." It wasn't because I pushed my religion or love for God on anyone. As a matter of fact, I would often be in seasons of denial, and doing my best to my relationship with the Lord.

No matter what I do or where I go, I can't hide it. My love for God oozes out of me in everything that I do. People see my compassion and love, but it's God.

Luke 7:47 KJV

"Wherefore I say unto thee, Her sins, which are many, are forgiven; for she loved much: but whom little is forgiven, the same loveth little."

God forgave me of so much. I turned my back on Him so many times, yet His love kept reaching out to me. The truth is I have always rebelled against the unique call on my life. I wish I could say I that wasn't true, however, that's not the case. Even now when I hear preachers talk about rebellion, it's a hard pill to swallow. I never put myself in that category. Even though it was true, it wasn't intentional. Thank God He knows our hearts.

A person with a peculiar call on their life always carries a unique burden. You didn't ask for the call. Sometimes you want it to go away. Sometimes you want to be normal like everyone else. I was born the daughter of a preacher, but never grew up with my Father. My Mom later became a preacher too.

I wanted to be young, carefree, and normal like everyone else. This calling followed me everywhere. It was in everything I did. Whether it was my friendships, dating, job, or even in my family, I tried to shake it, but couldn't.

Luke 12:48 KJV

"But he that knew not, and did commit things worthy of stripes, shall be beaten with few stripes. For whomsoever much is given, of him shall be much required: and to whom men have committed much, of him they will ask the more."

I remember a time in my early 20s when I was still vacillating in my friendships. I did this in my teens as well. Everybody wants friends. Even if you are a believer, you oftentimes don't care if they are believers, you just want acceptance and understanding. I had not accepted my call at that time, and to this day, I still struggle with accepting it.

This one particular time I went to the grocery store to buy some alcohol. While in the liquor aisle, I bumped into my Mom's friend. He was a Pastor. He said to me, "Aren't you in the wrong aisle?" I was so embarrassed and angry at the same time! All I could say was, "No." I was thinking, "God I can't go anywhere."

Now, looking back, I can see. It was God's hand and divine protection in my life. Every time the adversary tried to sift me; God was there battling on my behalf.

Luke 22:31-33

"And the Lord said, Simon, Simon, behold, Satan hath desired to have you, that he may sift you as wheat: But I have prayed for thee, that thy faith fail not: and when thou art converted, strengthen thy brethren."

God has kept me through so much. I'm not sure if I can write about it all. At 19, I started hanging out and partying on college campuses. One night, a lady I met who lived near me invited me to a revival meeting in her basement. I decided to attend and an older white woman in her 40s or 50s was speaking.

I can't even remember what she spoke about, but when she called for prayer, I went up. She began to prophesy. "You have been through things worse than a 40-year old." I started crying and I couldn't stop. Nobody knew that—not even my own family.

Later, the woman gave me her number and I called her. She started prophesying again and gave me instructions. She said, "Start to journal every day. You are going to have a tremendous hope ministry." She kept saying, "Tremendous, tremendous, tremendous" and she went on and on.

I haven't seen, heard from, nor spoken to that woman since that day. I can't even tell you her name. At the time I didn't understand what she prophesied to me, nor why, so I didn't start journaling…yet I believed her. I was young and too busy following the crowd. I needed to mature spiritually and become disciplined before I started my practice of journaling.

It was 1993. Even though I had not started journaling, I never forgot one word that woman prophesied to me. I'm sure this was because I inherited a photographic memory from my Father. He preached without notes. At the end he would say, "Lord, bless my bones." Knowing this makes me laugh, but I didn't find this out until after he passed.

I've always been someone that sees and hears things. I have seen so much that I learned to pretend not to see and hear as a defense mechanism. I can see someone's intention and heart may not be the best, yet I learn to love them just the same. Oftentimes I pretended not to see things because most times, I didn't want to. I've always believed the best about people.

I always recall conversations, facts, and situations. This made dating and relationships very challenging. For example, if something happened or someone said something, I would remind them.

When that woman prophesied about my ministry, that was memorable and profound, and her words would come back to my mind at different times. I now know God was nudging me into purpose and 20 years later, I am finally stepping into it.

I share this to let you know just how much God cares about you! Allow me to reveal an experience with you that happened to me in 2001. I never told a soul about what happened until 2018 when I was in a program getting my coaching certification.

I had an opportunity to present a workshop on digital marketing. I was speaking to coaches and business owners. It was at this time that God reminded me of the prophetic experience I had in 2001, and my life started to make sense. The chaos, rejection, and warfare started to make sense too.

This is a message the adversary didn't want to get out, BUT GOD! It's special delivery for the Body of Christ. It withstood all assassination attempts and has been divinely protected.

My life has had painful, excruciating, and crushing experiences. Most times I wanted to run and hide, but no one ever knew how I felt. My Pastor didn't know, my Mother and family didn't know (despite the fact that we were close), and I never told a soul. I couldn't and now I know why—God was protecting it for such a time as this.

My love for singing led me on a journey to worship. Worship led me on a journey to prayer. Prayer led me on a journey to intercession. Interceding for others and the Body of Christ is what brought this revelation to you.

In 2001 I worked as a secretary at my church. I was a part of the 5:00 a.m. intercessory prayer team. At lunchtime I would go into the sanctuary and pray. One particular day I went into our purple colored sanctuary to pray. As I bowed my knees on the first row to hit the floor, I closed my eyes.

Immediately after, here's what happened:

God took me into a room and showed me all the wealth in the world.

He said, "Do you see this?"

I couldn't speak. I was so overtaken. It was beautiful! It was the brightest, purest gold I had ever seen! It was glowing, shining, and weighty. Immediately, I became overwhelmed with humility and awe. I looked around and took it all in while I attempted to find the strength to give God a reply.

Before I could speak, I heard him say:

"None of it compares to my glory. I am Lord over Economic Kingdoms!"

The words kept ringing in my ear:

"Lord over Economic Kingdoms!" "Lord over Economic Kingdoms!"

I was speechless and started to weep. I couldn't stop. It was so humbling. The peace of God, his awe and wonder, filled my soul. I was so weak afterwards and I couldn't tell anyone. Then, I forgot.

It felt like the visitation described in the New Testament. Before John the Baptist was born, an Angel of the Lord visited his father in the temple. The angel revealed his soon-to-be son's name. When the angel left, John's father could not utter a word until the appointed time.

No, I didn't see an angel. I saw the WEALTH OF THE WORLD! Even typing it does something to me. It answers so many questions. It appeared as a physical place holding all the world's wealth. Even now I can't describe it. God wrote it on my heart and tattooed it in my spirit.

When I finished praying, I got up with a deep sense of knowing. A stillness and confidence filled my soul. Nothing can replace God's blessing and presence. God wasn't showing me the wealth.

In that moment God allowed me to see the world's wealth in comparison to Him. He then downloaded in my spirit a new revelation of his name, "Lord of Economic Kingdoms."

I had never heard that name or term. I hadn't heard it since—until 2018 when I gave my presentation. I sought God on what to do with this revelation. I agonized over it. I suffered because of it. I wrestled with it for years without telling a soul. Until now.

Let's review two passages of scripture below:

Psalms 24:7-10

"Lift up your heads, O ye gates; and be ye lift up, ye everlasting doors; and the King of glory shall come in.

Who is this King of glory? The Lord strong and mighty, the Lord mighty in battle.

Lift up your heads, O ye gates; even lift them up, ye everlasting doors; and the King of glory shall come in.

Who is this King of glory? The Lord of hosts, he is the King of glory. Selah."

Revelation 21:9-27

"And there came unto me one of the seven angels which had the seven vials full of the seven last plagues, and talked with me, saying, Come hither, I will shew thee the bride, the Lamb's wife.

And he carried me away in the spirit to a great and high mountain, and shewed me that great city, the holy Jerusalem, descending out of heaven from God, Having the glory of God: and her light was like unto a stone most precious, even like a jasper stone, clear as crystal; And had a wall great and height, and had twelve gates, and at the gates twelve angels, and names written thereon, which are the names of the twelve tribes of the children of Israel.

On the east three gates: on the north three gates: on the south three gates: and on the west three gates.

And the wall of the city had twelve foundations, and in them the names of the twelve apostles of the Lamb. And he that talked with me had a golden reed to measure the city, and the gates thereof, and the wall thereof.

And the city lieth foursquare, and the length is as large as the breadth: and he measured the city with the reed, twelve thousand furlongs. The length and the breadth and the height of it are equal.

And he measured the wall thereof, an hundred and forty and four cubits, according to the measure of a man, that is, of the angel.

And the building of the wall of it was of jasper: and the city was pure gold, like unto clear glass.

And the foundations of the wall of the city were garnished with all matter of precious stones. The first foundations was jasper; the second, sapphire; the third, a chalcedony; the fourth, an emerald; The fifth, sardonyx; the sixth, sardius; the seventh, chrysolyte; the eighth, beryl; the ninth, a topaz; the tenth, a chrysoprasus; the eleventh, a jacinth; the twelfth, an amethyst.

And the twelve gates were twelve pearls: every several gate was one of pearl: and the street of the city was pure gold, as it were transparent glass.

And I saw no temple therein: for the Lord God Almighty and the Lamb are the temple of it.

And the city had no need of the sun, neither of the moon, to shine in it: for the glory of God did lighten it, and the Lamb is the light thereof.

And the nations of them which are saved shall walk in the light of it: and the kings of the earth do bring their glory and honour into it.

And the gates of it shall not be shut at all by day: for there shall be no night there.

And they shall bring the glory and honor to the nations into it.

And there shall in no wise enter into it anything that defileth, neither whatsoever worketh abomination, or maketh a lie: but they which are written in the Lamb's book of life."

The revelation of the **"Lord of Economic Kingdoms,"** transformed my life. It set me on the journey of a lifetime. It cost me my reputation, friends, dear relationships, opportunities, and turmoil.

It reminds me of a conversation I had with God in my late 20s. The Spirit of God was so high, and I remember telling God, "Yes." I kept saying, "yes, Lord, yes." At the time, I believed I was surrendered to His will. Now looking back, my perspective has changed. I now call it the "Before and after yes."

It's the 'yes' before you know what's required to sacrifice and give up. It's the 'yes' *BEFORE* God reveals his plan. The 'naive yes' before you have the 'Job' experience. Then, there is the *AFTER* 'yes'. This is the 'yes' after the breaking and crushing. It's the 'yes' after you've experienced the humiliation.

It's the 'yes' after friends and family scandalize your name. It's what Jesus meant when he says, "Rejoice when men persecute you and say all manner of evil against you falsely". It's a 'yes' birthed from the depths of your soul. Looking back, I don't regret it one bit.

Throughout this book, we will discuss how to partner with **the Lord of Economic Kingdoms.** It's time to experience new dimensions of His dominion, wealth, and ownership. We will review the following concepts:

1. No Flesh Allowed
2. Value of the Glory
3. The Weight of Glory
4. Treasures in Earthen Vessels
5. Get in the Glory Flow
6. Claiming Your Inheritance
7. Thy Kingdom Come

If you've been believing for an economic breakthrough, this book is for you! Are you praying asking God for transgenerational wealth? You are perfectly positioned. Will you let God use you? Will you say, "Yes?"

No Flesh Allowed

After I had this life changing experience, I wondered why, but I had no clue. I didn't even question why the Lord blessed me with the gift of seeing. I always supported my Pastor and ministry. I knew the vision of the house, so I believe God was giving me a glimpse into what He had prepared. I didn't understand the weight of what I saw. It was years before anyone was talking about the coming wealth transfer.

I went back to business as usual. I had my own plans. I wanted to be a singer. I was already writing songs for the kingdom. God was giving me transformative songs for the Body of Christ in my personal prayer time. I was on a mission to fulfill God's divine plan for my life, or so I thought.

During times of worship, God used me in profound ways. He would speak to me about things I couldn't articulate to anyone. Here's an example.

I recall a dream I had during this time. It scared me, and I never told a soul. Now I know it was the adversary planting seeds in my mind to provoke fear. *The enemy knew who I was before I did.*

Here's the dream:

I was speaking and preaching somewhere, and someone came to the altar to give their life to God. It was a transvestite. The person came to give their life to God. They said it was because of me and wanted prayer.

I was so scared and religious that I didn't want the transvestite to touch me, so I ran. The further I ran, the darker it got in my mind. It was so dark. Then, I felt this overwhelming darkness to the point of almost losing my mind. Then, I heard angels singing and I woke up.

When I woke up, I felt fear all around. I didn't know how to interpret the dream. I also didn't want to talk about it. I never told anyone. Now, after discovering my purpose, I completely get it.

Sometimes God wants to use us to bless others, but we are so concerned about our safety and image. Sometimes we are so scared of how it will make us look that we shrink back. You can't run from the purpose(s) of God. If He wants to use you, He will. The further I ran, the darker it became.

I mentioned earlier that I didn't think running from my purpose was rebellion. I thought I had a choice. I am single and I grew up in a single parent household. I thought I could make my own decisions about my life. The idea to run my plans by the Father first never dawned on me.

When I prayed, I prayed for others. When I prayed, it was always about other things. Now, I see how powerful prayer is. I see how prayer can produce the results for anything you need. At 27, I didn't and couldn't see that.

I gravitate to young people. I encourage them to follow their dreams. According to scripture, most young people have zeal, but not according to knowledge (Romans 10:2). Paul admonishes the older women to teach the young (Titus 2:3-4). This is a sidebar but quite necessary. We need women of God who will take the young, unchurched who don't know and give them the tools they need to succeed.

So back to my dream. I was running from purpose. I ran from being in the front. I ran from being a potential target. At the time, I wasn't concerned about the darkness. I wanted to get away from it all.

Now, I can see how he enemy attempted to blind my mind. He wanted me to focus on the dream as opposed to what God was revealing. The angels singing and music at the end of my dream was God's way of bringing me back to His purpose for my life.

Music was all I knew. That's how everyone identified me. Friends called me "Songbird." When people see me, they ask, "Are you still singing?" God was reassuring me in the dreams He would still get the glory.

God was also teaching me that Lonna as I knew her, had to die to self. There were parts of my nature and character that couldn't go into the new realms of glory God desired.

1 Corinthians 1:23-31 KJV

"But we preach Christ crucified, unto the Jews a stumblingblock, and unto the Greeks foolishness; But unto them which are called, both Jews and Greeks, Christ the power of God, and the wisdom of God.

Because the foolishness of God is wiser than men; and the weakness of God is stronger than men.

For ye see your calling, brethren, how that not many wise men after the flesh, not many mighty, not many noble, are called:

But God hath chosen the foolish things of the world to confound the wise; and God hath chosen the weak things of the world to confound the things which are mighty; And base things of the world, and things which are despised, hath God chosen, yea, and things which are not, to bring to nought things that are:

That no flesh should glory in his presence.

But of him are ye in Christ Jesus, who of God is made unto us wisdom, and righteousness, and sanctification, and redemption:

That, according as it is written, He that glorieth, let him glory in the Lord."

No Flesh Shall Glory in "HIS" Presence!

I don't care who you are or what you do. I don't care how many degrees you have in front of or behind your name. I don't care how long you've been saved or in ministry. It doesn't matter if your name is in lights and known around the world.

NO FLESH WILL GLORY IN HIS PRESENCE!

I must admit, at the time, I didn't understand the severity of where I was. I couldn't have located myself in the Spirit if you told me. I was doing everything right. I worked at my church. I sang on the praise team. I supported my Pastor. I was on the intercessory team. I even drove the church van to pick people up from to time. No flesh can glory!

I was a youth administrator, choir director, and coordinated conferences. I served as the board secretary and more. No flesh will glory.

It wasn't about my title or my position. It wasn't about what I'd done for God. It wasn't even about what He showed me. It was about the Father's business!

God calls us to His kingdom and uses us for His glory. So many love the glamour of the glory. So many seek the glory. The glory is glorious and full of beauty. The glory is full of light. It's shiny. It draws. It attracts. Guess what? It belongs to God!

I didn't steal God's glory on purpose. I never looked or asked for the credit. I wanted God's will. The problems is...it was out of my own ability. I was born charismatic because my Father was charismatic.

I knew the word of God. I had a sphere of influence in my church and circle. God was making my name great by association. Serving was about Him and His kingdom only. No flesh will glory!

I had no clue of the correction, chastening, and breaking that was coming. The oil of God would materialize in my crushing. I was oblivious to the persecution I would go through. I fought it. I resisted so hard. I did everything to keep my life as I knew it intact. I wanted things to stay as they were.

Then, it happened. It was 2002. I helped coordinate a youth conference at my church. A dear friend helped. She didn't go to our church, but she was always a blessing to me. She had been in and out of the hospital for years fighting Lupus.

Her health was fine while coordinating the conference. Sometime during the conference, she ended up hospitalized. She was fighting for her life. I remember fasting and believing God for her recovery. She was in the hospital for about three days and was released. I was so relieved, and life went on as usual.

Within a week or two, she was back in the hospital. I was worn out from everything that was happening. My car broke down. I remember feeling so depressed. I couldn't get out of bed. Then I called and found out my friend was back in the hospital.

I wanted to go see her, but at the time, I didn't have transportation. She died shortly thereafter from the complications and surgeries. It was the beginning of a journey.

During this same time, I was dating a guy who was not very spiritual. I was so sad. He kept trying to comfort me and I remember telling him, "If that were my Mother, I wouldn't have left the hospital until she got up."

Shortly after, I had a dream. In it, my Mother was sleepy and tired. She was trying to go to sleep and lay down. I kept saying, "Mom you can't lay down here. You can't lay down." We were in front of a building that looked like a hotel. I sensed there were witches all around.

After I woke up, I couldn't shake the dream. On October 2, 2002, guess what? While teaching a bible study, my Mom suffered a brain aneurysm. Additionally, she had a stroke on both sides of her brain. I will never forget that day.

I hadn't talked to my mom in days. She had always suffered with high blood pressure. Some things happened in our family that week that upset her. My mom was so upset that she wasn't taking calls. This was not like her at all.

I remember it so well. The phone rang. I heard a voice telling me my mom was being rushed to the hospital. We didn't live in the same city. I lived about a half hour away.

When I arrived, my Mom was in the emergency room. She was getting ready to get sedated. She kept yelling at us to get her financials and find her insurance, but no one was listening. We were young, scared, inexperienced, and didn't know what to do. We didn't know what was going on.

Before the dream I shared earlier, my Mom also had a dream months before. She confided that she had dreamed about our family. We were on the basketball court playing ball. In the dream, she started to warn us, "A tornado is coming. A tornado is coming."

I wish I realized that God was trying to warn and prepare us. I didn't understand the gift of prophesy or the power of prayer. My Mother and I had a special relationship. We could talk about anything.

My mother was a very private person. She knew how to suffer in silence. When she did, she often would never say a word. We were so close. God would show me most things in a dream, and I would call her. After telling her what God had showed me, she would tell me what happened. These were things she hadn't told a soul.

After the brain aneurysm, she spent five months in the hospital. She ended up intubated. She was in critical care for three long weeks. Then, she spent the next five months in rehab.

After short term nursing care, and all was said and done, she ended up needing 24-hour care. Then, we received news of her long-term diagnosis. Doctors said it was vascular dementia. She also lost her ability to walk after being in the hospital for such a long time.

The entire experience devastated our family. Our mom was our rock. To this day, we are still healing. At the time, she was only 52. God taught me so much during this time. He increased my faith. He taught me about healing and healthcare. He showed me why it is important to always show up and be who he created you to be.

You make a difference. Your presence makes a difference. What you bring to the Body of Christ makes a difference. Somebody's life is depending on you to show up every time, no matter the opposition.

The bible tells us that, "In the world ye shall have tribulation: but be of good cheer; I have overcome the world." (John 16:33) Most don't realize that suffering and tribulation is part of the glory making process.

Remember I told you earlier "No flesh shall glory in his presence." It is in the death, burial, and resurrection process that God's power shines. You can't always see it until you get to the other side.

Later that same year, my uncle died. Then, my Mama "G" (a woman who I had been very close to for years and a strong believer in Christ) died. I became isolated, lonely, sad, angry, and resented my calling. I started losing people and things left and right. I needed a place of rest and break from it all.

I was a young, single woman. When I came home at night, I was alone. All I had time to do was think. No one knew what was happening. I didn't talk to very many people. We were still dealing with the aftermath of my Mom being back home and our family's new reality. I wanted someone and something to call my own.

I poured my heart and life into the church. At the time, I felt I had nothing to show for it. I was always on the giving end. I gave my heart. I gave my time. I gave my talents. My faith and trust in God began to shift. I completely forgot all the promises and things God had showed me. I didn't even think about it.

This is what the enemy does to so many believers. He attempts to take us off focus and get us to lose sight of **'The glory'**.

Hebrews 12:2 KJV

"Looking unto Jesus the author and finisher of our faith; who for the joy that was set before him endured the cross, despising the shame, and is set down at the right hand of the throne of God."

Our adversary uses many tactics and devices to throw us out of purpose and off track.

2 Corinthians 2:11 KJV

"Lest Satan should get an advantage of us: for we are not ignorant of his devices."

In this world of technology, we have to be especially vigilant. It's interesting, the enemy has been using devices for years to distract and steal from the people of God. If the enemy can keep you focused on immediate distractions instead of what's ahead (God's purpose), he will do so. This is his strategy to make you forget your identity in God.

After these series of events occurred, I started feeling empty. I felt like something was missing, since most of the relationships that undergirded me for so long were gone. I didn't realize that God was calling me to a higher place of glory and maturing me.

2 Corinthians 3:14-18 KJV

"But their minds were blinded: for until this day remaineth the same vail untaken away in the reading of the old testament; which vail is done away in Christ.

But even unto this day, when Moses is read, the vail is upon their heart.

Nevertheless, when it shall turn to the Lord, the vail shall be taken away.

Now the Lord is that Spirit: and where the Spirit of the Lord is, there is liberty.

But we all, with open face beholding as in a glass the glory of the Lord, are changed into the same image from glory to glory, even   as   by   the   Spirit   of   the   Lord."

Value of the Glory

I wasn't ready to go from milk to meat. The sad part is, I thought I was already on meat. God knew better. I had to learn that obedience is everything. At the time, I didn't think I was being disobedient, despite the fact that I was walking away from and out of God's will. I was living life by my emotions and feelings, as opposed to staying in faith. I was calling the shots without seeking God in all things.

I wanted to numb the pain. I started dating a musician from out of town. He was a preacher's son. I was running away from my calling and into it at the same time. I fell into fornication and found myself a single mother raising my daughter alone. This was something I had been through and never wanted to put another human through.

Shortly thereafter, my Father received a diagnosis. The doctors said he had a different form of dementia. I found myself being a caregiver for both my parents between the ages of 27 and 33. I walked away from my passion to sing, moved back home, and found myself working from home to balance it all.

At the time, I felt forgotten. I felt bamboozled, hoodwinked, and fooled, yet something very vital was happening. God's glory was being manifested in my life. His undeniable, overcoming grace and power was pulling me through. When others rejected me, God picked me up. He dusted me off again and again.

I could not shake all I had been through or what I had seen. During that time God planted so much in my spirit. I started to understand generational wealth and its power. The things my Mother spent her life working on for us started to make sense. God was teaching me about the cost and value of His glory.

Romans 5:1-3 KJV

"Therefore being justified by faith, we have peace with God through our Lord Jesus Christ:
By whom also we have access by faith into this grace wherein we stand, and rejoice in hope of the glory of God.

And not only so, but we glory in tribulations also: knowing that tribulation worketh patience;..."

Later on in the book of Romans, Paul tells us more about the glory:

Romans 8:18

"For I reckon that the sufferings of this present time are not worthy to be compared with the glory which shall be revealed in us."

Paul is showing us exactly what the glory looks like again and again:

2 Corinthians 11:30 KJV

"If I must needs glory, I will glory of the things which concern mine infirmities."

2 Corinthians 12:1-12

"It is not expedient for me doubtless to glory. I will come to visions and revelations of the Lord.

I knew a man in Christ above fourteen years ago, (whether in the body, I cannot tell; or whether out of the body, I cannot tell: God knoweth;) such an one caught up to the third heaven.

And I knew such a man, (whether in the body, or out of the body, I cannot tell: God knoweth;)

How that he was caught up into paradise and heard unspeakable words, which it is not lawful for a man to utter.

Of such an one will I glory: yet of myself I will not glory, but in mine infirmities.

For though I would desire to glory, I shall not be a fool; for I will say the truth: but now I forbear, lest any man should think of me above that which he seeth me to be, or that he heareth of me.

And lest I should be exalted above measure through the abundance of the revelations, there was given to me a thorn in the flesh, the messenger of Satan to buffet me, lest I should be exalted above measure.

For this thing I besought the Lord thrice, that it might depart from me.

And he said unto me, My grace is sufficient for thee: for my strength is made perfect in weakness. Most gladly therefore will I rather glory in my infirmities, that the power of Christ may rest upon me.

Therefore I take pleasure in infirmities, in reproaches, in necessities, in persecutions, in distresses for Christ's sake: for when I am weak, then am I strong.

I am become a fool in glorying; ye have compelled me: for I ought to have been commended of you: for in nothing am I behind the very chiefest apostles, though I be nothing.

Truly the signs of an apostle were wrought among you in all patience, in signs, and wonders, and mighty deeds."

So many people want God's presence, they want His anointing, but they don't want His glory.

Romans 8:4-8 KJV

"That the righteousness of the law might be fulfilled in us, who walk not after the flesh, but after the Spirit.

For they that are after the flesh do mind the things of the flesh; but they that are after the Spirit the things of the Spirit.

For to be carnally minded is death; but to be spiritually minded is life and peace.

Because the carnal mind is enmity against God: for it is not subject to the law of God, neither indeed can be.

So then they that are in the flesh cannot please God."

Are You Willing to Pay The Cost For Glory?

God's glory costs something. His glory is weighty and heavy. Countless individuals want cars, fame, status—temporary things. Yet, they run from the suffering, persecution, tribulation, and shame. Carrying the glory brings persecution.

The glory is significant, and it can kill you if you handle it the wrong way. Ask the ark of the covenant bearers attempting to bring it back to Israel. Specifically, ask Uzzah the son of Abinadab.

The glory of God is nothing to play with! It was so strong and powerful that the children of Israel begged Moses to speak to God on their behalf. It costs to live in His glory!

Once you experience God's glory, you'll want more of it. When it overshadows you, everything else is meaningless and secondary. There is nothing like the power and glory of the Living God. It is abiding, resounding, residing, and rich.

The glory of God is pure, holy, transforming, and alive. It is priceless, irreplaceable, and invaluable. You cannot buy it, trade it on the stock market, or devalue it. It possesses eternal value and significance, whether exchanged in heaven or in earth and you can take it to the throne room and cash it in at any time!

If you're reading this book, I'm 99.9% confident you were born to be a glory carrier. The glory brings distinction. Every prominent person in the bible made a name for themself bringing the tangible glory of God. They carried it everywhere they went.

Think about it. Whether Abraham, Isaac, Jacob, Moses, or Joshua. What about Samson, King David, King Solomon, or even Daniel. How about Elijah, Ezekiel, Isaiah, or Jeremiah.

If we look at the New Testament, the pattern still continues. Look at Jesus Christ, the Apostles, Paul, or St. John. The glory of God was so strong on the Apostle John that political leaders banned him to exile. There God revealed the revelation of Jesus Christ.

Each of these Biblical characters had encounters with the Living God that changed their life. They saw a new dimension of God every time it unfolded. They were first-hand witnesses of His majesty, authority, power, and tangible presence.

The glory caused Abraham to leave his family and what was familiar. The glory led Moses to return to Egypt as a strong leader in his old age. The glory showed him heaven's pattern of the temple. The glory was so strong that New Jerusalem still mirrors what God showed him to this day.

The glory of the Lord let Joshua take possession of the land. It helped King David conquer the enemies of Israel and rule the kingdom. King Solomon ushered in a new level of God's glory. It gave the nation of Israel peace from their enemies' roundabout.

Each glory carrier captured a different characteristic of God's glory. Their stories still speak to us today. There is so much to say about this subject. What I saw in that moment of intercession and prayer was the immense magnitude of God's glory.

It captured the totality of all the world's wealth in comparison to His glory. Are you sure you really want the level of blessing the Lord of Economic Kingdoms brings? If so, are you willing to pay the   price?

What Exactly is the Glory?

Maybe you thought this book was about how to bring financial increase and wealth in your life. It is. God uses the base and foolish things of this world to confound the wise. God's kingdom is above the world's systems, so everything He does outlives, outlasts, and outshines it.

God is not into temporary fixes. God deals in dominion, subduing, and reigning. When He begins something, "It is finished." When He creates anything, "It is glorious and beautiful." He always does it bigger, better, and greater. God's wealth and magnificence is no different.

The nation of Israel went from slavery to freedom, then returned to captivity. This happened several times in the old testament. Yet Israel still emerged as one of the world's wealthiest nations again and again. Why do you think they are so hated? Why do you think they have so many alliances? Do you think people align with them because **'they'** believe they're best people in the world? No!

People want to know more about the God of the Israelites. They wonder about their success and want their secret to wealth. Others see them dominating in every arena. They want that same thing even if they can't quite put their finger on what it is. It is more than ordinary wealth. It is the splendor and weight of the glory. This is how they are able to maintain wealth and it is how they capitalize off of it to create more.

The glory of God is a lasting, tangible differentiator. You cannot buy it. God chooses. He decides whether to rest His glory on a person, place, or thing. After all, He is God, and He is so very wise. He hides the dimensions of who He is. He conceals His kingdom and glory. A person has to be intentional about seeking it out.

God's glory reigns over all! Let me say it again. God's glory reigns over all. It reigns over economic systems. It reins over the banking industry. It reigns over financial markets. His kingdom reigns over central banking institutions. His kingdom reigns over the International Monetary System. His Kingdom reigns over the gross national and domestic product of every nation. God's glory reigns over all!

The Body of Christ must get this revelation. It is then that the Kingdoms of this world will become the Kingdoms of our God. In case you missed the memo, the kingdoms of this world HAVE ALREADY become the Kingdoms of our God (Revelation 11:15)!

We must take possession and return everything to the rightful owner. It is a finished work. It happened the day Christ led captivity captive and gave gifts unto men (Ephesians 4:8). Centuries later, the Body of Christ still hasn't taken dominion. Our limited perspectives have allowed the God of this world to blind our eyes to the truth and this stops now!

We can no longer look to systems, people, or temporary things to supply our needs. God, the author and finisher of our faith (Hebrews 12:2), supplies our needs. God is seeking such to worship Him in spirit and in truth (John 4:24). He is looking for true worshippers that know their dependency is on God. He is our source.

It is so important that we shift our thinking. The Word of God is already hidden in so many people's hearts. The problem is we are not talking about it and using it to create businesses and systems that reflect God's glory.

This is why Jesus shared:

Luke 16:8 KJV

"And the lord commended the unjust steward, because he had done wisely: for the children of this world are in their generation wiser than the children of light."

Rulers throughout history have created economic systems to govern people. In contrast, most of God's people have not been creating wealth and systems that mirror the Kingdom of God. There are a few born into families of wealth that think this way.

God instituted the principal of generational wealth and sanctioned it. We know this because we see what God started in Abraham. The promise of legacy and generational wealth is still evident in Israel today.

I remember in 2013 when God started dealing with me about generational wealth. He showed me the significance of the number three. God blesses a family with generational wealth in three generations. Then He establishes that family to be a blessing to the world. Let's look at Abraham, Isaac, and Jacob.

Genesis 22:18 KJV

"And in thy seed shall all the nations of the earth be blessed; because thou hast obeyed my voice."

God spoke to Abraham. Abraham hears and moves in obedience. God blesses him with a son named Isaac. Abraham circumcises Isaac and trains him in the ways of the Lord. Isaac has a son named Jacob, and we see the blessing is being transferred generationally.

Abraham told Isaac his story of faith. He shared what God showed him (the glory). He is building Isaac's faith. He is equipping Isaac to travel through unfamiliar territory looking for the promise. He is teaching Isaac how to hear and trust God.

Isaac knows the blessing is coming. He doesn't see it, but he is talking about. He is preparing his children to carry the blessing. He is teaching them what it looks and feels like to carry the glory. He is recounting it over and over again.

They are each making sure that each generation doesn't forget. They are ensuring each knows where they came from and where they are going to. They are saying things like:

- We started off a family, but are becoming a nation.
- We started off small, but our borders are expanding and enlarging.
- We started off wandering the earth, now we take possession of the promised land.
- We are creating a name for ourselves.
- We are creating everything we need to sustain us for generations to come.
- We are self-sufficient and don't need anyone else for anything.
- Everything we need is in our house.
- We lack nothing. We are a great nation. God's best belongs to us.
- Kings tremble because of our nation.

- No one can outnumber us. We are giants in the earth.
- Our enemies are our footstool. We have the necks of our enemies. They bow to us.
- God is with us!

Faith is working! Jacob grabs the blessing and promise, and He begins to wrestle with it. During the wrestling, he's transformed. At first, he works for Laban. He is working to make his own way. He is working to find a partner to build his generational legacy with. He is working to prove himself to his uncle and to bring God's promise to pass.

Then, after toiling, the blessing kicks in. He wins the wrestling match. His character is transformed. The angel assigns him a new name and reveals his true identity. He realizes like his father and grandfather that he has to stand on his own. Jacob claims his birthright. He leaves Laban's house and goes after what belongs to him.

This transformation of faith changes his name. He is no longer Jacob. Now, he is Israel. The blessing is happening. The promise is working through him. He is taking hold of the promise. He begins to be fruitful, multiply, subdue, replenish the earth, and have dominion.

Jacob, one man, multiplies into 12. One of his 12 children is Joseph. The 12 multiply into 70. The 70 become an entire nation. The rest is history and Israel is still standing today! It is the power of three and the power of the generational blessing working in a family's life.

God revealed to me the power of three. It takes three generations to see transformative change in a family. Part of the problem that exists in families is separation and division. Very few families can work together long enough to make substantive change in the earth. Many are too busy arguing about who is the leader. Some seek God for themselves, but not for the entire family.

When God showed me this, it changed my prayer life. He told me when I pray to cover no less than three generations, our entire family and bloodline. It was another form and level of intercession. It no longer was only about me. It was about our family. It was about our future.

What would our family look like if no one had to go into debt to buy a house or go to college? What would it look like if no one was without healthcare or hardship due to a medical condition? What would our family look like if everyone had a place to live? What if every family member had somewhere to go in their old age? What if the glory of God rested on our families?

This is the reason I started my business, Live Your Song LLC. My Mother worked all her life as a businesswoman in the 70s when it wasn't popular to be a woman in business. She sacrificed so much for us. She brought us up in the Word of God as a single Mother, making sure we stayed in church. She bought land to prepare us for our future.

When she had her brain aneurysm, she lost everything she worked for. She lost her business, land, ability to walk and pray on her knees. It looked like she had lost it all, except, she was a wise woman. She was a God-fearing woman. She was a woman of faith and she had planted a seed.

My Mom's seed grew in the garden of faith. The garden began to flourish, producing good things. Trees grew deep roots and began to branch out. The branches began to feed everything that needed sustaining. The garden started growing in size and stature, and now, it multiplies exponentially .

I call it the generational multiplication factor. Let's focus on Abraham again. Abraham stepped out on faith. He sowed his seed, and it produced a seed named Isaac. Isaac stepped out on faith. He resowed the seed and it produced two (Jacob and Esau). Jacob stepped out on faith. He resowed the seed and it produced 12. The 12 turned into 70.

I am not a mathematician, but I want you to see there is no clear-cut formula on how much the glory of God will produce. It didn't double with each generation; it exceeded that. Once you get to the third generation, it exceeds the law of exponential growth.

$$2^3 = 2 \times 2 \times 2 = 8$$

If we look at what took place in three generations only applying the law of exponents, the answer would be eight. Israel had 12 sons, which supersedes that. This means a higher law kicked in—God's law.

The law of glory governed by the Lord over Economic Kingdoms. This law surpasses the natural laws governed by man. It overtakes the law of duplication, multiplication, and exponential growth governed by man. It dominates, outdoes, and outnumbers them.

I am God. I can do anything I please!

God plans for us to move and grow exponentially as a part of His kingdom. He wants us to supersede everything that has come before us. He wants us to produce more, do more, and become more.

St. John 14:12 KJV

"Verily, verily, I say unto you, He that believeth on me, the works that I do shall he do also; and greater works than these shall he do; because I go unto my Father."
This means you can't "Do you!" You can't look at your life through your one-dimensional lens. You must consider the sacrifices of those who have gone before you.

Do you know how many persecuted saints there have been? Do you know how much bloodshed happened so you can carry the glory? In America, we often honor the history of our country. We talk about all the victories we've won and how proud we are to represent the greatest country on earth.

What about the Kingdom of God?

How should we represent God? How proud are we of the rich history of His Kingdom? How proud are we of the way the disciples and saints fought for the glory and power of the Kingdom? What did they have to sacrifice so we could have the Word of God centuries later? The same Word that is still transforming hearts and lives today. What did Jesus' disciples pay for the glory?

The glory remains. The glory quickens. The glory makes alive. The glory makes whole. The glory brings rest. The glory of God is unstoppable, unflinching, unchanging, invincible, and untouchable. It is the realm where the Living God resides and dwells.

First, we need to work on uniting families. We need to mend family relationships. We need to put families back in order again. We need to think about generational wealth:

- What sacrifices do we need to make as a family?
- What stories do we need to recount and retell?
- Where have we been as a family?
- Where are we going as a family?
- What were we called to this earth to do as a family?
- What is the family blessing?

After we answer these questions and unify as a family, then we need to pray for our generations and bloodline:

- Pray for healing for previous generations.
- Pray the family blessing for generations.
- Use your prayers and daily conversation to bless your family.
- Speak life over your family.
- Keep the good things going. So many spend too much time talking about what's wrong in the family. Bless and curse not.

When you pray, call your name and bloodline out before the Lord. Don't only think about your immediate household. Think about your ancestors, aunts, uncles, cousins, nieces, nephews, and future generations. See your family's role in context to God and the Body of Christ.

Here are more questions to ask:

- What role does salvation play in your family?
- What is God's position in your family's life?

- How does God want to manifest his eternal weight of glory through your family?
- How will future generations remember your family?
- How will your future generations look?
- What will your future generations produce in the earth?
- What can you do right now to start being fruitful and multiply?
- How will you take dominion?
- What areas of your family and bloodline do you need to subdue?

Another example of a kingdom economy principle at work is in the book of Job. Here's how the first chapter describes him:

Job 1:1-3, 5 KJV

"There was a man in the land of Uz, whose name was Job; and that man was perfect and upright, and one that feared God, and eschewed evil.

And there were born unto him seven sons and three daughters.

His substance also was seven thousand sheep, and three thousand camels, and five hundred yoke of oxen, and five hundred she asses, and a very great household; so that this man was the greatest of all the men of the east.

And it was so, when the days of their feasting were gone about, that Job sent and sanctified them, and rose up early in the morning, and offered burnt offerings according to the number of them all: for Job said, It may be that my sons have sinned, and cursed God in their hearts. Thus did Job continually."

In the first chapter Job starts by going to God on his family's behalf. Scripture tells us he sanctified his family before the Lord after they sinned. He rose early and offered burnt sacrifices for each. Job did this again and again.

As a result of Job's sacrifices, faith, and prayers, God recognizes Job and identifies these qualities in Job. God is glorying in his servant Job. He is excited about Job. He is well pleased. How do we know this? Satan didn't mention Job's name. God did.

Job 1:8 KJV

"And the Lord said unto Satan, Hast thou considered my servant Job, that there is none like him in the earth, a perfect and an upright man, one that feareth God, and escheweth evil?"

The Lord of Economic Kingdoms is ready to showcase and show out in Job's life. He's ready to put his servant on display. He points out four qualities in reference to Job:

- There is none like him in the earth.
- He is perfect (complete, mature, healthy).
- He is upright (straight, right).
- He fears God.
- He eschews or flees from evil.

Satan began to dialogue with God, questioning Job's dedication and faithfulness. He used the same tactics he's been using against mankind for generations. He starts focusing on the blessings.

I'm paraphrasing. Well, God you did put protection around him. Didn't you? You know what else? You did bless the work of his hands. Didn't you? Look at his substance and how his land has increased. Why don't you test him? See what he does then.

Satan tried the same trick with Jesus in the garden.

Matthew 4:8-10 KJV

"Again, the devil taketh him up into an exceeding high mountain, and sheweth him all the kingdoms of the world, and the glory of them;

And saith unto him, All these things will I give thee, if thou wilt fall down and worship me.

Then saith Jesus unto him, Get thee hence, Satan: for it is written, Thou shalt worship the Lord thy God, and him only shalt thou serve."

It didn't work then, and it didn't work with Job.

God doesn't flinch in His resolve. He already knows what is to come. Nothing can compare to "His glory!" God is quite confident that because of Job's trust in Him, he can trust Job in return.

Job withstands the test. After turmoil, loss, devastation, isolation, and persecution, he breaks down. Job says this:

Job 19:6-27 KJV

"Know now that God hath overthrown me, and hath compassed me with his net.

Behold, I cry out of wrong, but I am not heard: I cry aloud, but there is no judgment.

He hath fenced up my way that I cannot pass, and he hath set darkness in my paths.

He hath stripped me of my glory, and taken the crown from my head.

He hath destroyed me on every side, and I am gone: and mine hope hath he removed like a tree.

He hath also kindled his wrath against me, and he counteth me unto him as one of his enemies.

His troops come together, and raise up their way against me, and encamp round about my tabernacle.

He hath put my brethren far from me, and mine acquaintance are verily estranged from me.

My kinsfolk have failed, and my familiar friends have forgotten me.

They that dwell in mine house, and my maids, count me for a stranger: I am an alien in their sight.

called my servant, and he gave me no answer; I intreated him with my mouth.

My breath is strange to my wife, though I intreated for the children's sake of mine own body.

Yea, young children despised me; I arose, and they spake against me.

All my inward friends abhorred me: and they whom I loved are turned against me.

My bone cleaveth to my skin and to my flesh, and I am escaped with the skin of my teeth.

Have pity upon me, have pity upon me, O ye my friends; for the hand of God hath touched me.

Why do ye persecute me as God, and are not satisfied with my flesh?

Oh that my words were now written! oh that they were printed in a book!

That they were graven with an iron pen and lead in the rock for ever!"

For I know that my redeemer liveth, and that he shall stand at the latter day upon the earth:

And though after my skin worms destroy this body, yet in my flesh shall I see God:

Whom I shall see for myself, and mine eyes shall behold, and not another; though my reins be consumed within me."

This is where the wealth or glory transfer happens!

Job lost everything he had—including all 10 of his children. Everything he depended on or prided himself in was gone. Friends walked away. He had lost his reputation. He had lost the familiar and his comfortable place. He suffered persecution, but he pressed through it all declaring, "I will still see God!

Psalms 139:8 KJV

If I ascend up into heaven, thou art there: if I make my bed in hell, behold, thou art there.
By the time we get to Job 42, Job as surrenders. Once he does this, the tide changes. God is ready to spotlight Job in an even greater way than before. He is ready to show him another dimension of glory. Look what happens:

Job 42:7-17 KJV

"And it was so, that after the Lord had spoken these words unto Job, the Lord said to Eliphaz the Temanite, My wrath is kindled

against thee, and against thy two friends: for ye have not spoken of me the thing that is right, as my servant Job hath.

Therefore take unto you now seven bullocks and seven rams, and go to my servant Job, and offer up for yourselves a burnt offering; and my servant Job shall pray for you: for him will I accept: lest I deal with you after your folly, in that ye have not spoken of me the thing which is right, like my servant Job.

So Eliphaz the Temanite and Bildad the Shuhite and Zophar the Naamathite went, and did according as the Lord commanded them: The Lord also accepted Job.

And the Lord turned the captivity of Job, when he prayed for his friends: also the Lord gave Job twice as much as he had before.

Then came there unto him all his brethren, and all his sisters, and all they that had been of his acquaintance before, and did eat bread with him in his house: and they bemoaned him, and comforted him over all the evil that the Lord had brought upon him: every man also gave him a piece of money, and every one an earring of gold.

So the Lord blessed the latter end of Job more than his beginning: for he had fourteen thousand sheep, and six thousand camels, and a thousand yoke of oxen, and a thousand she asses.

He had also seven sons and three daughters.

And he called the name of the first, Jemima; and the name of the second, Kezia; and the name of the third, Kerenhappuch.

And in all the land were no women found so fair as the daughters of Job: and their father gave them inheritance among their brethren.

After this lived Job an hundred and forty years, and saw his sons, and his sons' sons, even four generations.

So Job died, being old and full of days."

We visited a lot of scriptures, and each word was necessary. Now I want to highlight several points:

- The friends who were speaking against Job and the plan of God for his life fell out of favor with God. His wrath was kindled against them.

- These same friends could not bring an offering to God because of this. They had to go through Job. God uses this situation to give Job authority.
- Job prays for his friends. The same heart of humility he has toward God, he now has to exercise and extend to his friends.
- The Lord of Economic Kingdoms begins to pour His glory on Job in a greater way.
- After Job was healed, his brothers, sisters, and family start coming together to celebrate him.
- Everyone at the celebration has to bring Job something of value in exchange for the glory. They brought money and gold.
- Everything that was taken from Job was returned with supernatural increase.
- After Job's 10 children were killed, Job had 10 more children (7 sons and 3 daughters), except this time each daughter's name is documented.
- There were no women found so beautiful as Job's daughter. Each daughter received an inheritance which was not the norm.
- Job lives four generations to see his increase and blessings.

Let's do some quick math.

10 children X 10 dimensions of glory = 100-fold increase!

This is what the glory of God looks like when all said and done. It comes **during** the transfer **after** the trials. It comes **after** the persecution and tribulation. Here's what I want you to hone in on.

After it is all said and done, his three daughters now have respect, recognition, and reverence. They have their inheritance in the kingdom.

Daughters or women conceive the vision of the house. Daughters carry vision. They protect vision. They birth it too. They carry and birth the seed, so it is multiplied in the earth.

Earlier we talked about the power of the number three.

Three daughters each representing three different things. It is so significant that their names are recorded. Women's names were only recorded in the bible if they made or changed history. If a woman's contribution the family lineage was significant, it was recorded in memory. Job's daughter's names were:

- **Jemima,** which means dove.
- **Kezia,** which means Cassia.
- **Kerenhappuch-Keren** meaning "horn of light" and happuch "the horn or child of beauty"

Here the glory manifests in three distinct ways:

- Rest - Doves represent peace and the Holy Spirit.
- Resources - Cassia was a sweet-smelling spice. Today, it called cinnamon. It was an ingredient given to Moses to include in the recipe for holy oil. It was also used in trade and had great value. Greeks even used Cassia to make wine. Wine brings happiness, overflow, blessing, and joy. It is still used today in Jewish culture to honor the Sabbath.
- Riches - The ray of light and beauty reflects God's goodness in the earth. It attracts honor. It is NOT physical money alone. It brings wealth, grace, healing, salvation and whatever else you need.

So many are praying for the glory, but don't understand why all hell is breaking out around them. You are a glory carrier! God desires to get His glory out of you, so do not be confounded nor ashamed.

Isaiah 61:6-7

"But ye shall be named the Priests of the Lord: men shall call you the Ministers of our God: ye shall eat the riches of the Gentiles, and in their glory shall ye boast yourselves.

For your shame ye shall have double; and for confusion they shall rejoice in their portion: therefore in their land they shall possess the double: everlasting joy shall be unto them."

Make it a priority to read the entire chapter of Isaiah 61. I am sure you have read it several times. This time, I want you to see it with a new perspective. This time see it describing the glory. It outlines:

- The purpose of the glory.
- The signs of the glory.
- The benefits of the glory.
- The mantle of the glory.
- The fruitfulness of the glory.

Releasing the Glory

Once we submit to God's glory and see it, we will see it for our family. We will see it for our friends. We will impact our communities to change the world around us.

We can then put systems in place to create cultures that bring heaven to earth. God showed me this at a very young age. It was prior all hell breaking out in my life. I'll never forget it. I was in my late 20s talking, about what I am sharing with you today. This was before my Mom's accident.

Like my Mom, I have always been a giver. When God gave me this revelation, I assumed it was for church, while up front leading service. I remember I would drive by one particular church every day. Up the street was a nursing home. God downloaded an idea into my spirit and I set up a meeting with the Assistant Pastor to share it.

So many in the Body of Christ were getting sick but didn't have healthcare or anyone to take care of them long term. Many sowed their lives believing God and giving to the ministry.

What if the church started a mutual fund so families could invest $5 a month? What if they could build an investment mechanism to plan for their loved one's future? This was 20 years ago. What if this money could go into a bigger pool creating compound interest to help? When the time came for long-term care, financial support would be accessible.

It wouldn't be typical nursing home care. Loved ones would get physical and spiritual care. The importance is that their faith and spiritual regimen wouldn't interrupted. Essential workers would pray, read scripture, and provide real healing to them. They would receive proper nourishment for their body. Families could ensure their loved one was getting the holistic care they needed.

I'll never forget the conversation. The assistant Pastor looked at me like I was crazy. The conversation never moved past that meeting. I'm not quite sure why I even thought he had that level of faith. I guess it was because he was the Assistant Pastor responsible for souls and others spiritual care.

After I left, I was so convinced that I shared what God showed me to the right church for the right congregation. It was one of the biggest multicultural churches in the city. Looking back, I should have prayed about it first. The Lord of Economic Kingdoms can show you where to sow your gifts, time, and resources.

In the kingdom, faith is currency. We've heard this for a long time. Dr. Bill Winston (who I respect) says it all the time. The problem is many have the currency of faith, but are not investing it in the right type of ground. I am chief sinner in this.

When God unveiled the revelation of Him as Lord of Economic Kingdoms, I was blown away. I began asking why He allowed me to see that revelation. I wondered why He shared it with me. He reminded me of two prayers I prayed in my early 20's:

- **Lord Let me bring forth 100-fold**
- **Lord I want to give you the high praise and ride upon the high places.**

Let's examine each.
100-fold Increase

Matthew 13:1-10 KJV

"1 The same day went Jesus out of the house, and sat by the sea side.

2 And great multitudes were gathered together unto him, so that he went into a ship, and sat; and the whole multitude stood on the shore.

3 And he spake many things unto them in parables, saying, Behold, a sower went forth to sow;

4 And when he sowed, some seeds fell by the way side, and the fowls came and devoured them up:

5 Some fell upon stony places, where they had not much earth: and forthwith they sprung up, because they had no deepness of earth:

6 And when the sun was up, they were scorched; and because they had no root, they withered away

7 And some fell among thorns; and the thorns sprung up, and choked them:

8 But other fell into good ground, and brought forth fruit, some an hundredfold, some sixtyfold, some thirtyfold

9 Who hath ears to hear, let him hear.

10 And the disciples came, and said unto him, Why speakest thou unto them in parables?"

1. Good Ground

I prayed for God to let His words fall on good ground in my heart and life. In this passage, Jesus speaks to his disciples in a parable. Since these two prayers, my life has been a parable. I could not understand why certain things were happening. I knew I had a prayer life. My faith was so high that I expected immediate results!

Now, I know it was because I prayed these prayers. I wasn't asking for something temporary or a quick fix. I wasn't asking for material possessions. I asked God to cultivate my heart and life to be able to carry His glory.

God can only use us when we completely yield to Him. Sometimes there are areas of our lives we yield, and others we do not. When we first receive salvation and believe, we may increase at a 30-fold production rate. Our belief is according to our hunger and desire for His word.

As we mature, we may increase to a 60-fold production rate. Here we may pray, believing for others, and even worship in a greater way. But the 100-fold increase is a different story. This is saying to the Lord, whatever Jesus was able to do, I want to do. I want to increase what he did and more! I want to take up my cross and follow you, trusting you will supply everything I need.

Think about it. Jesus called the disciples. They could have chosen to stay in their comfortable place by the tree or shore. Instead, when the King of Glory called, they followed him. They recognized his ability to sustain them. They saw his ability to feed them. They knew he could calm the storms. They detected his potential hidden power to be Lord of Economic Kingdoms.

Here's the key. Your heart has to be good ground. There's a tilling process for every harvest. No matter what, this process has to happen. It even happens if your heart is good ground and you produce. Each time you harvest, the tilling happens again. In the

41

Kingdom of God, we're called to be fruitful, plenteous, and multiply all the time.

Think about it. When Jesus called the disciples, they could have chosen to stay by the tree or on the shore. Instead, when the King of Glory called, they followed him. They recognized his ability to sustain them. They saw his ability to feed them. They knew he could calm the storms. They detected his potential hidden power to be Lord of Economic Kingdoms.

The tilling and crushing process is where the glory of God happens. Dr. Tiffany K. Jordan says it best, "We have to allow the Father to process and perfect us." Patience has to have its perfect work (James 1:4). Through faith and patience, we realize the promise. When the process is painful and it hurts, that is when we learn to worship the deepest and praise the most."

Until recently, I didn't even understand the value of His glory. As a child, I heard about the parable of the talents all the time. The focus was always on the man who didn't use his talent. Even greater, was the fact that he hid it in the ground.

The problem wasn't coming because he hid it in the ground. That's what you do with a seed, you put it in the ground. He put it in the "Wrong ground!"

The problem was the ground he put it in. It wasn't producing. The ground wasn't bringing forth. He should have inspected it first, prayed over it, and tilled it. We, as the servants of God, must always ask the question, "Is the ground good for growing conditions?"

In this instance, I am not speaking of the condition of your heart or life. *You* are a seed! I am speaking of your love, your ministry, your gifts, your business, and everything else God has given you. Do some reflection and ask yourself. After all I've invested, do I see a return on investment (ROI)?

Over the next 30 days, think about your faith. Reflect, pray, and answer these questions:

- What am I believing God for?
- What works have I produced that match what I'm believing for?
- Where have I sown or invested?
- Is this the type of ground I should be investing in?

- If the answer is yes to any of the questions above, where is my increase?
- If the answer is no to any of the questions above, what will I do about it?
- What is the value of what God has given me to the Body of Christ?
- What systems am I called to build or change?
- What does a return on my investment look like to God and to me?

The Lord of Economic Kingdom wants to bless you and your family. Governing with his glory requires a new mindset.

St. Matthew 9:17 KJV

Neither do men put new wine into old bottles: else the bottles break, and the wine runneth out, and the bottles perish: but they put new wine into new bottles, and both are preserved.
Jesus had this mindset. He expected ROI when he showed up. It's why he was dominating everywhere he went. He could multiply anything!

He could show up and turn water to wine. He could bring coins out of a fish. He was Lord of Economic Kingdoms. They were calling him King before he ever introduced himself. He showed up and commanded tangible glory to come.

St. Mark 11:12-14 KJV

12 "And on the morrow, when they were come from Bethany, he was hungry: 13 And seeing a fig tree afar off having leaves, he came, if haply he might find any thing thereon: and when he came to it, he found nothing but leaves; for the time of figs was not yet. 14 And Jesus answered and said unto it, No man eat fruit of thee hereafter for ever. And his disciples heard it."
Jesus spoke to the tree and said, 'May no one ever eat fruit from you again.' His disciples heard him say this. That's one reason he was so

angry. When they came back, the tree had not produced what they needed.

Jesus was hungry and hadn't had any rest. The resource was not available when he needed it. Afterward, he headed to the temple. Tired and hungry, he sees the money changers selling products."

Of course, I'm speculating on exactly why he was angry. He knew the temple was close. Is there food in the temple? Are the people of God praying? Is the church being fruitful? Do they have what I need? Why isn't this tree multiplying? It is in proximity to the church!

When he and the disciples come back to the tree, it is completely dried up. The disciples had a look of astonishment, but Jesus wasn't surprised at all. He looked at that tree with boldness. He declared, "You won't ever deceive anyone into believing you'll produce again!"

God's glory was at work. He was revealing himself as Lord of Economic Kingdoms.

2. The High Praise and Ride Upon My High Places

As I shared, I am a worshipper. I grew up in church giving God praise. It wasn't until I was older and read this passage that this became a part of my request:

Isaiah 58:1-14 KJV

1 "Cry aloud, spare not, lift up thy voice like a trumpet, and shew my people their transgression, and the house of Jacob their sins.

2 Yet they seek me daily, and delight to know my ways, as a nation that did righteousness, and forsook not the ordinance of their God: they ask of me the ordinances of justice; they take delight in approaching to God.

3 Wherefore have we fasted, say they, and thou seest not? wherefore have we afflicted our soul, and thou takest no knowledge? Behold, in the day of your fast ye find pleasure, and exact all your labours.

4 Behold, ye fast for strife and debate, and to smite with the fist of wickedness: ye shall not fast as ye do this day, to make your voice to be heard on high.

5 Is it such a fast that I have chosen? a day for a man to afflict his soul? is it to bow down his head as a bulrush, and to spread sackcloth and ashes under him? wilt thou call this a fast, and an acceptable day to the Lord?

6 Is not this the fast that I have chosen? to loose the bands of wickedness, to undo the heavy burdens, and to let the oppressed go free, and that ye break every yoke?

7 Is it not to deal thy bread to the hungry, and that thou bring the poor that are cast out to thy house? when thou seest the naked, that thou cover him; and that thou hide not thyself from thine own flesh?

8 Then shall thy light break forth as the morning, and thine health shall spring forth speedily: and thy righteousness shall go before thee; the glory of the Lord shall be thy reward.

9 Then shalt thou call, and the Lord shall answer; thou shalt cry, and he shall say, Here I am. If thou take away from the midst of thee the yoke, the putting forth of the finger, and speaking vanity;

10 And if thou draw out thy soul to the hungry, and satisfy the afflicted soul; then shall thy light rise in obscurity, and thy darkness be as the noon day:

11 And the Lord shall guide thee continually, and satisfy thy soul in drought, and make fat thy bones: and thou shalt be like a watered garden, and like a spring of water, whose waters fail not.

12 And they that shall be of thee shall build the old waste places: thou shalt raise up the foundations of many generations; and thou shalt be called, The repairer of the breach, The restorer of paths to dwell in.

13 If thou turn away thy foot from the sabbath, from doing thy pleasure on my holy day; and call the Sabbath a delight, the holy of the Lord, honourable; and shalt honour him, not doing thine own ways, nor finding thine own pleasure, nor speaking thine own words:

14 Then shalt thou delight thyself in the Lord; and I will cause thee to ride upon the high places of the earth, and feed thee with the heritage of Jacob thy father: for the mouth of the Lord hath spoken it."

The glory that allows you to walk the earth in the authority of the Lord of Economic Kingdoms requires a different lifestyle and sacrifice. It is not just something you do on Sunday, or when you bow your knees to pray.

It is a lifelong commitment. It is allowing God to use you as a light helping the poor and naked. It is a glory that crushes the head of oppression. If you noticed, it even deals with how you treat your family. It's an entirely new thought process and way of living. It defies religion:

James 1:27 KJV

"Pure religion and undefiled before God and the Father is this, To visit the fatherless and widows in their affliction, and to keep himself unspotted from the world."

So many want the glory. Yet, it only shows up when they are standing in the sanctuary or sitting in the pulpit. Some want to lead their perfect lives, never getting their hands dirty or wet with others tears. That's NOT God.

In scripture, we see Jesus pouring his life out in service to others. He's preaching the gospel to the poor. He's on a mission. Can you image if he only came for the Jews? Where would we be?

I remember attending a church and the Pastor's wife escorted a woman to the front of the church with her two children. Whatever had happened before then was a blessing. I can't remember exactly why she was calling her up now.

I saw what happened next with my own two eyes. She began to tell their story and about the blessing. I can't even remember what she said next. I only remember the following line: "When they came in, this family reeked of poverty."

What? Are you kidding me? How is that possible? How do you say something like that in front of an entire congregation and their children? How do you think that mother felt when she left? How do you think she explained the experience to her children? I am sure it wasn't intentional, but it doesn't matter. It's not the heart of God!

God cares about the poor, lost, and hurting. He cares whether people have food on their table. God cares!

St. James says it like this:

James 2:14-19 KJV

14 "What doth it profit, my brethren, though a man say he hath faith, and have not works? can faith save him?

15 If a brother or sister be naked, and destitute of daily food,

16 And one of you say unto them, Depart in peace, be ye warmed and filled; notwithstanding ye give them not those things which are needful to the body; what doth it profit?

17 Even so faith, if it hath not works, is dead, being alone.

18 Yea, a man may say, Thou hast faith, and I have works: shew me thy faith without thy works, and I will shew thee my faith by my works.

19 Thou believest that there is one God; thou doest well: the devils also believe, and tremble.

20 But wilt thou know, O vain man, that faith without works is dead?"

Are we even reading our bible? Come on man!

We are the church!

We are the sheep of HIS pasture!

We are HIS workmanship!

We're supposed to reflect Jesus in the earth. We've read a lot of scriptures. I'm holding back on breaking this down. It needs to more depth and teaching. If you read the entire passage of scripture, it speaks about being a "Respecter of Persons"(Acts 10:34) which God hates.

How are we comfortable treating people (God's people let me add) any kind of way? We must do better if we are to carry His glory!

I was praying for the 100-fold increase, the high praise, and to ride the high places. Each level requires a dying and a giving of yourself. You can praise God with your lips all day long, but it's the position of your heart that He is after.

Isaiah 29:13 KJV

"Wherefore the Lord said, Forasmuch as this people draw near me with their mouth, and with their lips do honour me, but have removed their heart far from me, and their fear toward me is taught by the precept of men."

Some may say, "well this is "Old Testament." This scripture appears many times throughout the word of God. Jesus quotes it himself. The glory of God requires a sacrifice of your heart and life.

Money Is Only A Medium of Exchange

There are levels and ways of giving. Money is only a medium of exchange. When God revealed what he showed me in prayer, seeing Him as the Lord of Economic Kingdoms became clearer. My Mom had already had her brain aneurysm and I was a single Mother.

I kept thinking about how my Mom lost everything. More than that, we almost lost her. We couldn't even take care of her. She needed 24-hour 7-day a week around the clock care. I kept thinking if only I was in a better place I could do more.

With that, I had a beautiful little girl looking up at me with her bright, brown eyes. I felt I had failed and missed the mark. I kept thinking about how I could honor my Mother's legacy to leave an inheritance for my child.

At the time, my daughter was two or three years old. I started to travel around the country to learn everything I could about wealth. I looked for like-minded believers burning with a desire to see God's vision for His body fulfilled.

I became a member of an organization dedicated to helping grassroots organizations. It was for those who wanted to act as "Ambassadors for Christ." I was high in faith.

Every month, I drove to Florida to meet others from around the world. We heard the word of God, learned how to prepare for wealth, and worked on a detailed plan. I will never forget those days. I learned so much and I saw the unbelievable.

It was 2008. A man we called Brother D. taught us the inner workings of wealth. It was mind blowing! Some concepts were so deep that I couldn't share them if I tried.

One experience which sticks out for me was when Brother D. was teaching us on the real value of money. He pulled out a $20 bill. Then, he pulled out a $2 bill. He started teaching us how deceptive the world's monetary system is. He said, "Don't you know these are both printed on the exact same .02 cent paper?

I was in complete shock. I'd never even thought about that. He then explained how they originated from the exact same place. This stuck with me. So much so it's 12 years later. I'll never forget it.

Money is a medium of exchange. That's it. It's the value we place on it that gives it significance. It is printed, exchanged, used, and circulated based on perception. We perceive it to have more power than it actually does.

Because of this false perception, the God of this world hath "blinded their minds (2 Corinthians 4:4)." The Body of Christ and world suffers as a result. People have put money where the "Lord of Economic Kingdoms" should be.

I'll never forget Brother D. The things I learned and saw were life changing. The organization met at different locations around the country and I'll never forget the time we met in Atlanta.

It was on a Sunday morning and it was our final day of training. Everyone was getting ready to leave to make their flights to return home. Brother D. didn't speak often. He called us back into the room and told everyone to close the door.

I was out in the lobby saying goodbye to friends. When I saw the doors closing, I ran back inside. I stood at the very back. He then warned whoever wasn't serious needed to leave. I had no clue what he was about to say.

He said, "We're about to pray." He instructed us to repeat after him. He first made us pray a prayer of repentance. Then with the most powerful voice I've ever heard, he started to cast out demons. He came against "High mindedness" and "Self-exaltation." I will never forget that prayer.

The next thing you know people began to cough around the room. He continued. He started to pray against the "Prince of Persia" and others. I don't remember all of the names. I was in my early thirties at the time, and with all my life experience in church, I had never heard this type of prayer.

Then he said something that I don't remember, but he put his hand in the air as if to grab something. He called for wealth, took the blood and foot of Jesus, stomped and said, "I crush the serpent's head." Something in the room broke.

When I woke up the next morning the stock market had crashed. Everyone on the news was talking about real estate and bad loans. If I hadn't seen it with my own eyes, I would not have believed them. I saw the power of God move in a way I've never seen in my life.

If one man's faith can do that, what else can praying people on one accord do to shift the economy? That level of authority requires a glory and lifestyle only God can give. I'm not sure what sacrifices he had to make or lifestyle he had to live to gain that level of spiritual insight.

What I do know is that high mindedness and self-exaltation run rampant in the church. If I hadn't heard those words with my own ears, I would never have made the connection. At times, I find myself repenting from it because it's easy to get caught up in believing you are more than you are.

When these times happen, God will remind you, "I'm still running this. I'm still in control." He won't share His glory with another. So, let's examine the word *glory*.

For the purpose of this book, we will use the definitions of glory that are below:

- Garment, glory, goodly, mantle, robe.
- Ornament: beauty, bravery, comely, fair, glory, honour, majesty.
- Literal brightness; ceremonial purification; clearness; purifying.
- Splendor, beauty, comeliness, excellency, glorious, goodly, honour, majesty.
- Grandeur
- To shine; hence, to make a show, to boast, to celebrate.
- To celebrate, commend, (deal, make).
- To be heavy or to make weighty .
- Renown

- Superbness
- Magnificence, majesty, mighty power.

As you can see, the glory comes in many different manifestations and dimensions. You can "taste and see that the Lord" (Psalm 34:8) is good. There's so much more to the glory. You can experience God again and again and each time you'll learn or see something new.

God's glory is so powerful, mighty, splendid, bright, magnificent, and weighty. Once He allows you to wear his mantle of glory, you become an ornament in His house. You are able to shine and attract attention. People begin to celebrate you. They want to be close to his majesty and purity.

Wearing God's glory is a heavy calling. You can't put it on or take it off whenever you like. You must remain cloaked in Him.

Sometimes you may want to go off on someone. You may want to backbite, gossip, tell your side of the story, or prove someone wrong. There may be times when you want to party, have fun, or let your hair down. Sometimes you'll want to have a few cocktails to forget who you are, relax, and fit in. Trust me I've tried each.

The Lord of Economic Kingdoms won't allow you to do any of that. What you carry inside of you is not about *you*, it's about *Him*. Sometimes what someone carries

is more valuable than their own life. Ask Jesus!

You cannot carry God's glory anywhere you choose. God gives you direction and permission on where to take His glory. He has to authorize your movement, because there is a weight to the glory. It rules over all, and has to rule you too.

Moving The Weight

Moving The Weight

One of the words used to describe God's glory is weighty. There is a weight to carrying the glory. When I first had my daughter, I gained 80 pounds. I was so big. I remember walking places. People would ask me, "Are you having twins?" It took everything in me not to cuss them out and go off. I was having a hard time carrying the extra weight.

I could hardly breath. I couldn't fit into the clothes I used to wear. Even when I sang my voice changed. It was much lower. The baby I was carrying required me to feed her even when I didn't feel like eating. If I didn't eat when I was hungry, I would get nauseous. I loved fish, but I couldn't eat any fish while I was pregnant. This baby had me eating a lot of beef.

My appetite completely changed. My body composition morphed too. I was becoming a completely different person. I was so ashamed of the extra weight. This made me depressed and withdrawn. I lost passion for going places, seeing people, and doing the things I used to do.

As I became older, my hormones started changing. The weight became harder to get rid of. Eating the same food I used to eat when I was younger had a completely different effect on my body. I would tell friends how much I wanted to lose weight. Many would stay, "You're still beautiful. You are not that big."

In the meantime, I felt something completely different. I felt the weight. I wasn't the same. From the outside looking in, it may have appeared I was. I loved to dress, and I love beautiful things. I didn't feel I could express my true self.

This is an example of how it feels to carry God's glory:

- You are carrying someone else inside.
- You have to feed it even when you don't feel like it.
- You don't fit.
- You're no longer able to do the things you used to do.

- Your appetite changes.
- You are no longer the same.
- You become someone else.

Jesus commands us to die to ourselves, take up our cross, and follow him. The cross is weighty. You can't get to the glory until you carry your cross and die. You have to die to expectations. You have to die to imaginations. You have to die to your past. You have to die to the person you thought you were. You have to die to yourself.

The road to glory is the road to surrender. It is the road to crucifixion. It is also the road to resurrection. The road to resurrection is the road to glory, and glory trumps all:

Hebrews 12:1-2 KJV

1 "Wherefore seeing we also are compassed about with so great a cloud of witnesses, let us lay aside every weight, and the sin which doth so easily beset us, and let us run with patience the race that is set before us,

2 Looking unto Jesus the author and finisher of our faith; who for the joy that was set before him endured the cross, despising the shame, and is set down at the right hand of the throne of God."

Endure these present sufferings and afflictions for a light moment so you can get to the glory. Go through the pain. Go through the humiliation. Go through family and friends that persecute you. Go through loved ones walking away. Nothing you endure can compare to the glory.

Guard the Glory

The glory can be very heavy. Sometimes you may want to take a breather. You may want to let your hair down and let it all hang out. In these times, you need good people around you that can guard the glory. God showed us this pattern set through the Holy of Holies:

Hebrews 9:2-5 KJV

2 "For there was a tabernacle made; the first, wherein was the candlestick, and the table, and the shewbread; which is called the sanctuary.

3 And after the second veil, the tabernacle which is called the Holiest of all;

4 Which had the golden censer, and the ark of the covenant overlaid round about with gold, wherein was the golden pot that had manna, and Aaron's rod that budded, and the tables of the covenant;

5 And over it the cherubim of glory shadowing the mercy seat; of which we cannot now speak particularly."

Cherubim and Seraphim angels guard the glory of God. His glory is so valuable. When Adam and Eve were in the garden, they carried this glory. They were unstoppable. They could do anything. They were in God's image walking the earth. When any creature, being, or entity on the face saw them, they saw God.

Imagine how Satan felt? God kicked him out of heaven where his only job was to worship the Living God who created everything. He wanted for nothing. He was second in command to none. Then, his passport was revoked and he was cut down to the ground (Isaiah 14:12). The dominion and authority he had while in right standing with God no longer existed.

When God cast Lucifer (Satan's name in heaven) out of heaven, he lost his authority, yet he convinced one-third of the angels to go with him (to reside in a place that was away from the presence of God). God saw him for exactly who he is (just like God sees us for exactly who we are). Lucifer said, "I will be like the Most High God" (Isaiah 12:14). When he was cast out of heaven, the angelic hosts realized he was a wanna-be god, yet one third chose to side with Satan. Satan was stewing and decided to devise a plan to war against God.

When Satan begins to derive a plot to come against God, who does he see? He sees God, and not only is He reigning in heaven, he's ruling the earth. Satan strategizes how he can get his place back, and Adam is the perfect target.

We know the story. God gave Adam one command. "Of the tree of the knowledge of good and evil you shall not eat, for in the day that you eat of it you shall surely die"(Genesis 2:17). Satan deceives Eve by twisting the Word of God, and she eats the forbidden fruit. She then entices her husband Adam to eat it, and he gives in (Genesis 3:1-7).

After disobeying God (sinning), the result was a death sentence (as God promised in Genesis 2:17). Yet, we still see the power in the glory of God at work. Adam and Eve are so saturated in it that God gives one command (I am paraphrasing), God says, "Guard the glory!" Let's take a deeper look:

Genesis 3:22-24 KJV

22 And the Lord God said, Behold, the man is become as one of us, to know good and evil: and now, lest he put forth his hand, and take also of the tree of life, and eat, and live for ever:

23 Therefore the Lord God sent him forth from the garden of Eden, to till the ground from whence he was taken.

24 So he drove out the man; and he placed at the east of the garden of Eden Cherubims, and a flaming sword which turned every way, to keep the way of the tree of life.

God immediately recognized that His glory was contaminated (the garden of glory), so He set Cherubims to guard and keep it. We must guard the glory. Whether through our conversations, covenant relationships, thoughts or everyday interactions. It is a must.

In the bible, hair represents glory. We see Samson full of strength and the glory of God to deliver the nation of Israel. Samson's fame traveled throughout the land. He could have any woman he wanted. All he wanted was a place to let his hair down.

Samson enjoyed having the recognition that comes with strength, but not the maintenance. Didn't everyone know that his long hair was too weighty? When it was hot, he had to pull it up. When it was wet, it became heavier. He wanted a safe place to let down his hair.

Delilah seemed like the perfect fit. She cared about his needs. She was so interested in only him. She wanted to know what made him tick. Unguarded and unaware, he let out the secret. God's glory was his strength. Delilah caught him off guard after much persistence, and he told her the secret to his strength (his glory). She cut him where it hurt him the most. She cut his glory. Now, the weight was lifted, but so was the glory.

God's children need to be surrounded by people who can cover us at all times. People we can be transparent with. People we can count on to watch our backs. People who will pray us through when needed.

We need people we can confide in. People that can provide a place we can go to let down our guard. We need those who know where it hurts, but will help our healing process. Peter says it this way:

1 Peter 4:8-10 KJV

8 "And above all things have fervent charity among yourselves: for charity shall cover the multitude of sins.

9 Use hospitality one to another without grudging.

10 As every man hath received the gift, even so minister the same one to another, as good stewards of the manifold grace of God."

When you have access to the glory, you have an endless supply. People see the hand of God on your life. They think they can have easy access whenever they want. It can seem attractive for someone to need or desire you at all times. It puts a person in power to know they can meet a need at any time. It can also be dangerous.

The key to remember is this. Glory is not yours. You can't give it out whenever you feel like it or whether you choose to or not. You cannot park God's glory anywhere you please. Everyone can't have access to you and the glory. Giving it to the wrong person can alter their future for decades. It can even cause them to touch it and leave the earth before their time.

Ask King David. Uzzah learned the hard way. Many know the story. The ark of the covenant was being returned to Israel. In the Old Testament, the ark represented a foreshadowing of the glory of God. Even then, God was showing himself as the Lord of Economic Kingdoms.

As David and his men moved the ark, they praised God with instruments and all their heart. The oxen stumbled. Without an invitation or instruction, Uzzah touched the ark or glory of God. As a result, he died (2 Samuel 6:6-7).

As a result, David decided not to bring the ark back to Israel. He parked it in Obed-Edom's house. The bible tells us that Obed and his household prospered. The ark or glory of God brings a tangible, noticeable, and distinct blessing to the entire house.

The Weight of Glory

We are to be "Glory Carriers." We are to establish, have, and generate Kingdom wealth in the earth. In order to do this, we have to know how to carry the glory. Drug dealers call this "moving the weight." We have to know how to transfer the glory from one spot to another.

As money is a medium, we must use God's glory as a medium of bringing about change. We must use God's glory to answer the call. We must use it to bring heaven to earth. The Lord of Economic Kingdom principles must begin to dominate and rule. They must not only dominate and exceed, but supersede the world's culture. They must dominate, rule, and control the wealth.

Wealth creates systems. Systems create kingdoms. Kingdoms give authority. Authority allows mindsets to reign and rule. We as the Body of Christ understand that "Power belongs to God" and He can give it to whoever he may choose.

Even if you live like a pauper you don't have to act like one. You don't have to beg anyone for anything. You don't have to allow this world's system to be your source and dependency. Last year, after all the revelation and the things I had seen, I had to make a decision.

In 2018, I stepped out on faith and quit my full-time employment. A few years prior, I went back to school to complete a Master's degree. My current job was in my field of study, and I made good money with bonuses.

At the same time, I worked two part-time jobs to fund the vision God put in my heart. One freelance client brought in more than one month's income. As I continued to invest in my business, I had to make a decision, so I took the leap and stepped out on faith.

After implementing a successful strategy, the client's work started to taper off. I started to get nervous. Then, God sent a major Silicon Valley client. He was positioning me for a Kingdom assignment. God began to bless me and give me divine favor. The client asked me to act as a spokeswoman for the company.

I received a promotion in every company I've worked in since my daughter was born. I would start in one position, then, they would see my skill set and offer me another position. This new client ended up doing the same thing.

I helped develop the initial implementation strategy. The specific strategy was to build a startup to tap into caregiving expertise. Do you remember the story I mentioned earlier where I shared what God told me with the Assistant Pastor? This company is now prospering and raising millions of dollars in investment seed.

After they started to expand, they brought on a large Philadelphia firm. I was advising the firm, answering questions, and executing parts of the strategy. As we began to collect more user data, the company started to change my role. They wanted me to be more out-front advocating on their behalf, with less pay.

Although the work would be less, I had to make a decision. Would I continue to put what God gave me on the back burner for someone else's dream? Would I devalue the gifts inside? I made a decision to end the contract.

Fast forward, I am out on the water of faith. Excited, nervous, and scared all at the same time. After all, I am a single Mother, what was I thinking? I started to panic. I needed a backup plan, or so I thought.

I started looking for a part-time job. I didn't pray about it. I didn't fast on it. I went and began looking. I found a decent part-time job. After months on the job, God's divine favor and glory was kicking in.

The company knew I already had a business. When I first started it, the organization evaluated my program. We provided after school services through the school system and we always received very high scores. As a result, they knew me in my role as a business owner. During the job interview, they spoke very well of our business and said I would be able to continue my business.

After two months on the job, things changed. The organization created an employee handbook. The company was in the same industry or ecosystem my business was in. God's favor began showing out in my life.

The organization approached me about signing a contract. They wanted me to agree that we wouldn't do business with any other organization in the city. These organizations were my main customers. After weeks of mulling it over, I had to make a decision.

I attended Joseph Business School's leadership conference. While there, I saw a picture of a beautiful woman. She was a presenter. Her session was, "Prayer that produces results." I was so drawn to her and I can't explain why.

I asked the person at the audio booth where her session was. She said, "You might not get a seat. Her sessions have been full to capacity." My daughter and I decided we would go and take a chance. We arrived late.

When we got there, it was full. There wasn't a seat available. We stood at the back of the room. My daughter was with me so I changed locations so she could get a better view. Within seconds, a gentleman offered his seat.

It was so timely and so God. There were other women standing all around. I had missed some of her presentation, but what I heard changed my life. She was a single Mother and God had instructed her to leave her job. She stepped out on faith.

It had been seven years and she hadn't looked back. God was sustaining her! I had been praying for over three years about this very thing. We even moved into a smaller place. I gave over two-thirds of everything we had away. I couldn't figure out how to do it.

One thing she said that stuck with me is, "God is your source. Everything else is a resource." I realized that although God had given me this revelation years ago, I hadn't been walking in it. I hadn't been seeking or seeing him as "The Lord of Economic Kingdoms."

I was praying about everything else but money. I didn't even talk about money. Seeing God as the source of everything causes everything else to bow. Money and material things must come into submission. Systems and governments must come into submission. His kingdom reigns!

Until this revelation gets in your soul and spirit, you can't walk in the realm of dominion to carry God's glory. It opposes everything we're taught. It goes against our nature. We seek security. God wants us to have security. He wants us to be our trust in Him. He is the best investment plan on the planet.

I'm not advocating you quit your job or stop what you're doing, but I do encourage you to stop letting fear control your decisions. You must carry God's glory into a system or sphere of influence.

You must not bow to the system; the system must bow to the God in you. He is the Lord of Economic Kingdoms. Can I get a witness?

Ask Noah. The earth was completely flooded. He started with the arc, his family, and animals and he is still making history. Ask Abraham. He left his father's house and ended up a nation. Ask Moses. He led the children of Israel out of Egypt with gold and wealth destined for the promised land.

Ask Joseph. He devised Egypt's resource distribution plan. He saved his entire family in the process. Ask King David, he killed Goliath, and later became known as the "Dancing King." He danced before the Lord.

Ask Jesus. He began his life receiving gifts from three kings. He turned water into wine and performed miracles everywhere he went.

Ask God:

Proverbs 13:22 KJV

22 "A good man leaveth an inheritance to his children's children: and the wealth of the sinner is laid up for the just."
God stores up wealth for the just. You can't tell me the glory is the same thing as the world's system. Israel is the example.

In every example I shared, one thing is clear. The economic systems that were created transferred from generation to generation. As a matter of fact, it still remains. This is an enduring glory. It is weighty enough to stand the test of time.

2 Corinthians 4:16-18 KJV

16 "For which cause we faint not; but though our outward man perish, yet the inward man is renewed day by day.

17 For our light affliction, which is but for a moment, worketh for us a far more exceeding and eternal weight of glory;

18 While we look not at the things which are seen, but at the things which are not seen: for the things which are seen are temporal; but the things which are not seen are eternal."

Are you ready to become a "Glory Carrier"? Will you step out in faith and trust the Lord of Economic Kingdoms? He is the subduer and supplier that cannot fail!

Things to consider:

1. What are you carrying inside?
2. What weights do you need to let go?
3. What do you need to feed?
4. What parts of self need to die?
5. What safeguards do you need to put in place?
6. Who needs to be in your life in this season?
7. How are they helping you guard God's glory?
8. What does being a "Glory Carrier" mean to you?
9. To whom, what, or where do you need to carry the glory to?

Treasures In Earthen Vessels

Glory is a peculiar thing. It comes in many different dimensions. It reveals itself in many distinct forms. It unveils itself in the most obscure places and things. Take for instance the diamond.

A diamond is one of the world's most precious stones. To discover it you have to mine it out. The jewel hides inside of rock and dirt. The rock is hard to find, as it is buried in a dark place deep within the earth's core. It is concealed even more, locked up in the earth's mantle.

What about pearls? Each are beautiful. Pearls are developed inside the shells of small living creatures. Living on the peaceful waters of the ocean, you find them in volcanic atolls or protected lagoons.

Treasures or gems must be sought out. They carry high value and worth. Their nature is to hide in unpredictable places. The glory they hold requires search and discovery. You see this pattern in any treasure, precious metal, or natural resource. Someone that finds precious gems is a gem collector.

Over time, they learn the skill of collecting gemstones. These stones bring notoriety, power, majesty, splendor, beauty, and wealth. Does this sound familiar? Each of these words describe a different aspect of God's glory.

The Lord of Economic Kingdoms is the greatest gem collector in heaven or on earth.

The heavens declare God's glory (Psalm 19:1). We see this demonstrated when God gives Moses instructions to build the temple. We also see this when we look at the instructions God gives for designing priestly garments. He had each priest decked and adorned with precious stones. God is into details.

Each precious stone or gem created reflects a unique vibrance and distinct character. They each show up in different colors. They show there is no limit to the brilliance and variance of God. As in heaven, so in earth:

2 Corinthians 4:6-7 KJV

6 "For God, who commanded the light to shine out of darkness, hath shined in our hearts, to give the light of the knowledge of the glory of God in the face of Jesus Christ.

7 But we have this treasure in earthen vessels, that the excellency of the power may be of God, and not of us."

In the Kingdom of God, up is down and down is up. God doesn't need to boast, show off, or make himself bigger than He already is. Have you heard the story of a discreet millionaire who interacts with others every day?

Rarely does anyone proclaim he or she is a person of wealth. Why? They are not trying to impress anyone or get anything. They already have everything they need. Can you imagine God going undercover? In actuality he did. He hid inside a baby wrapped in swaddling clothes.

Imagine the humility of God. He hides treasures and mantles in dark places. Most of the time unless you dig deeper, you will miss it.

God dealt with me about this years ago when I was working in a church. I observed people all the time. I directed the youth choir, so I met a lot of young people and their parents.

It was interesting to see those working behind the scenes. Most were kind, genuine people. They believed the church building was a place where family came together. They believed everyone took one for the team. There were also others as well.

I remember one time working in the kitchen helping to serve food. We had leftovers after a church dinner. The head of the kitchen fixed the pastor's children a plate and gave it to them. The children of a church Trustee saw it and also asked for food. The answer was no.

These young children had to sit there watching the other children eat. I'm sure they wondered what they had done to earn such special treatment. This type of thing has gone on in the church for too long.

No longer can we choose who does or does not get served at the table. The power of God fell in the book of Acts because "they were all with one accord in one place " (Acts 2:1). The church was prospering so much that they were adding to the church daily.

The bible is clear. Each member was getting exactly what they needed because the people "had all things in common" (Acts 2:44). For example, if someone has two cars and someone has none, the person who owned two would give one away. If someone had an empty bed in their home and the other had nowhere to go, the person with room would open up their home.

In those days, the church had a different mindset. The Acts church understood that God hides His "treasures in earthen vessels" (2 Corinthians 4:7) or people. We don't decide who carries the treasure, God does. We don't decide what package the treasure comes in, God does. He's the treasure maker.

On my journey to spiritual growth, God put people in my path to get me to a place of maturity. Some I knew for years. Some saw me grow and toil along the way. Others I met only once, yet, God still used them to get the glory out of my life.

Each could have passed me by, discarded the gift of God in me, and acted like what I was carrying didn't matter to the world. If they did, you wouldn't be reading this book right now. I would never have had the opportunity to realize the full potential of what God had for me to do in the earth.

It was a gradual process happening over the span of a lifetime. God was developing and growing the hidden treasure within. At times, I couldn't see or feel the treasure. I didn't even realize how valuable the gems were. Others saw it in me, but I couldn't see it in myself.

God, the great gem collector, saw fit to add me to His heavenly collection. As a result, I'm on full display. So are you. So is everyone who dares to "run with patience the race that is set before us"(Hebrews 12:1).

We must be delicate with God's people. They are precious. We don't know what they carry. They could be the next deliverer. There isn't a consistent outpour of Heaven's wealth yet for the Body of Christ. It's because the Body still acts fragmented and broken.

Let me preach and prophesy. No matter what it looks like or how it feels, we are "NOT" a broken body. Jesus Christ's bones were never broken. They pierced him in the side and water came gushing out.

He was the living water. The living waters of God has a flow. It's important that different members of God's body come together, connecting to flow in the glory of God. We can only do this if we begin to look, speak, and treat people as God created them. We are to be the glory and image of God.

God's glory comes in different shapes and sizes. The earth cannot contain it. Why do we try to mishandle and misjudge the glory of God? We are not qualified.

When understanding the principle of "hidden treasures," we must understand two things:

- God can use anyone He pleases.
- God, not man gets to choose.
- We don't get to dictate who or what God uses.
- We don't get to determine how God uses it.
- The instrument or earthen vessel God uses is for His glory alone.
- All vessels lead back to Him.

2 Timothy 2:20-22 KJV

20 "But in a great house there are not only vessels of gold and of silver, but also of wood and of earth; and some to honour, and some to dishonour.

21 If a man therefore purge himself from these, he shall be a vessel unto honour, sanctified, and meet for the master's use, and prepared unto every good work.

22 Flee also youthful lusts: but follow righteousness, faith, charity, peace, with them that call on the Lord out of a pure heart."

Another thing we must recognize about "earthen vessels" is that they are just that...earthen. We are clay filled with God's life, breath, and image. It sounds simple, yet we treat people like they are gods, bowing down to their whims and demands. I am chief sinner above all.

Did God say to do what you're doing? Did you seek Him first in all things? Are you living for God or for the people? Has your church become a social club only for the chosen few?

I believe God is not happy with the state of the present-day church in America. It's as if God is not welcome in His own home. More emphasis is on pleasing the masses rather than pleasing Him. We are not to "please" the masses, we are to "feed" the masses.

Proverbs 14:12 KJV

12 "There is a way which seemeth right unto a man, but the end thereof are the ways of death."

Proverbs 21:2 KJV

2 "Every way of a man is right in his own eyes: but the Lord pondereth the hearts."

I remember when God first started dealing with me about "a way that seemeth right unto man." I was born in Generation X. As a result, I have had an interesting time adjusting to the age of social media. Everyone is posting everything. Often at the detriment of others.

Being in business, I struggled because I didn't like taking pictures. I didn't like posting every detail of my day. I kept hearing you have to post to gain followers. I love people, yet it seemed so impersonal to me.

I started to feel left out. I would see others I admired posting pics. They were talking about their expertise and who they were. Many in my circle would say, "You need to put yourself out there more." My heart has always been to help others, lift others, and make others shine.

Then, one night God started dealing with me. He was waking me up all night. I kept hearing:

Acts 5:29 KJV

29 "Then Peter and the other apostles answered and said, We ought to obey God rather than men."

I kept trying to get back to sleep. God kept talking. He was talking so much I had to get up and find a pen and paper to take notes. He went on:

Galatians 1:10 KJV

10 "For do I now persuade men, or God? or do I seek to please men? for if I yet pleased men, I should not be the servant of Christ."

This hit me like a ton of bricks. I wasn't posting on social media because I cared more about how I looked to others than pleasing God. God called me to preach over 20 years ago. Until recently, I completely forgot.

Distracted, I was busy looking at what everyone else was doing. I hadn't taken the time to be still before the Lord. I needed to be able to hear His voice to recognize it. I needed His gentle leading. I shut down. I didn't want to deal with religion anymore. I was over it.

Growing up in church was all I knew. I felt I had nothing to show for everything I had given. I prayed for others' success, gave when I didn't have, and I felt like I had been hurt so much in the process.

Here's the thing. Heaven keeps great records. The beauty of God is this. He sees in secret and rewards you out in the open.

1 "Take heed that ye do not your alms before men, to be seen of them: otherwise ye have no reward of your Father which is in heaven.

2 Therefore when thou doest thine alms, do not sound a trumpet before the

Matthew 6:1-6 KJV

e, as the hypocrites do in the synagogues and in the streets, that they may have glory of men. Verily I say unto you, They have their reward.

3 But when thou doest alms, let not thy left hand know what thy right hand doeth:

4 That thine alms may be in secret: and thy Father which seeth in secret himself shall reward thee openly.

5 And when thou prayest, thou shalt not be as the hypocrites are: for they love to pray standing in the synagogues and in the corners of the streets, that they may be seen of men. Verily I say unto you, They have their reward.

6 But thou, when thou prayest, enter into thy closet, and when thou hast shut thy door, pray to thy Father which is in secret; and thy Father which seeth in secret shall reward thee openly."

It is not what we do when everyone is looking that matters. **This includes pleasing God.**

Pleasing God is a lifestyle and eternal work of glory. This is where the glory and wealth happen. God stores up good treasures for the called. He has a special account assigned to your name. He pays in residual dividends with compound interest.

Deuteronomy 12:12-13 KJV

12" The Lord shall open unto thee his good treasure, the heaven to give the rain unto thy land in his season, and to bless all the work of thine hand: and thou shalt lend unto many nations, and thou shalt not borrow.

13 And the Lord shall make thee the head, and not the tail; and thou shalt be above only, and thou shalt not be beneath; if that thou hearken unto the commandments of the Lord thy God, which I command thee this day, to observe and to do them:"

Pleasing God must become a lifestyle.

Please God first and in all things is a principle that goes against the norms of this world. This is especially true in business. In the world's economic system, they tell you to use data. Find out what will "please man" and then create it. It is also said to "make sure your business solves a problem."

Every business is not for every customer. This is great in theory and principle; however, God's economic order takes it a bit higher. God is the solution solver. Meaning he has identified the solution before the problem even arises. He is on the forefront of every great economic boom.

Let me elaborate.

I have had the pleasure of working in a remote setting for three well known Silicon Valley startups. Two turned into multi-billion-dollar ventures, and one is on its way. In each case, I had the opportunity to see each company in their infancy. My team helped grow and expand the company into new markets.

Here's an example:

While pursuing a Master's degree, I was working at home for Uber. When we started, they were only in six markets. I started in rider support. Operations would ask remote workers questions to pick our brains.

As a result of input, a small number of us received a promotion. We transitioned to the Uber Everywhere team. Our goal was to help expand the company from six small markets to over 354. This was half the U.S. While with the company, I received a promotion four times. I became an asset, identifying potential issues "before" they arose.

This trend followed me everywhere I went. I became very good at identifying systems and processes that needed to be more efficient . In most cases, the companies had not detected the problems at all.

The world's system says identify the problem, find a solution. God's economy says, "I am the solution for every problem." I can cite example after example of this pattern found throughout the scriptures.

Let's review:

Noah receives a warning from God that it is going to rain. God instructed him to build an ark, giving him specific instructions. Nobody believes, and it starts to rain and doesn't stop for 40 days and nights. Due to his obedience, Noah's saves his family.

Joseph dreams as a little boy. His brothers throw him into a pit and sell him as a slave. He ends up in prison positioned to interpret Pharaoh's dream. He warns of the coming famine. Pharaoh makes him second in command, and he saves an entire nation.

Moses is an orphan. He is taken to Egypt and disconnected from his people, culture, and ways. God raises and trains him inside of Pharaoh's house. He leaves the nation after killing a man. Over 40 years later, God sends him back to deliver his people out of bondage from Pharaoh and he leads them to freedom.

King David starts as a young, overlooked shepherd boy. He is training to protect sheep. After killing a lion and a bear, God uses him to take out Goliath. He protected God's people. God grooms him to be king. He later uses all the preparation to raise him as King of Israel. David's bloodline gives us the Lord Jesus Christ the reigning King over all.

Throughout time, the Lord of Economic Kingdoms has proven Himself. He has a pattern of getting ahead of the problem. He is a solutionist.

God Gets Ahead of The Problem

Earlier I mentioned Isaiah 58. I shared how I prayed for "100-fold increase" and to "ride upon my high places." When I was young, my mother planted this scripture in my heart. She said if I began to observe the Sabbath and practice this text, God would bless my music ministry. This was in 1994.

Like most children, I heard my mother but didn't act on it. I kept it in the back of my mind. Every time I read it, I looked at it from a different perspective, but I didn't put it into practice until years later.

It was at a time that I went through a very hard time in life. I had experienced church hurt so I wasn't attending church. I was streaming from home. I was faithful to the stream (laugh out loud), and I ended up in a relationship with a Muslim.

He chased me for three years. At a very weak moment I started listening to weak council and I opened a door that was very hard to close. I started seeking God and praying for forgiveness. I heard God tell me not to pursue the relationship. At the time, I thought I was being religious. I learned later, it was in fact God speaking loud and clear.

Afterward I was so broken. I started seeking God. I decided I needed to get back to the basics. I began revisiting the ten commandments. I knew so much scripture. I had been in church all my life. I spent my early adult years serving powerful ministry with deep revelation.

I knew the word of God but felt I had become "so spiritual minded that I wasn't any earthly good." I started to cry out to God and thought, "Lord, I want to get back to the basics."

As I began to read the commandments, I assessed where I was. I examined each one by one. When I started to review the following text, it hit me like a ton of bricks:

Exodus 20:8-11 KJV

"Remember the Sabbath day, to keep it holy."

Six days shalt thou labour, and do all thy work:

But the seventh day is the Sabbath of the LORD thy God: in it thou shalt not do any work, thou, nor thy don, nor thy daughter, thy manservant, nor thy maidservant, nor thy cattle, nor thy stranger that is within thy gates:

For in six days the LORD made heaven and earth, the sea, and all that in them is, and rested the seventh day: wherefore the LORD blessed the Sabbath day, and hallowed it."

The scripture in Isaiah 58 my mother shared with me over 20 years earlier came to mind. I started meditating on what God was showing me. As I continued to seek the Lord about what I was hearing, he started speaking. He brought the following passage to mind:

Hebrews 4:9-16 KJV

"There remaineth therefore a rest to the people of God.

For he that is entered into his rest, he also hath ceased from his own works, as God did from his.

Let us labour therefore to enter into that rest, lest any man fall after the same example of unbelief."

Some would argue that this is an Old Testament saying, and we are no longer bound under the law. At the time I shared this with a few loved ones, and they said the most interesting things. Some felt I had departed from the faith. Looking back, this is hilarious. It demonstrates why there has been stagnation moving into the things of God. God doesn't think that small.

I'm glad I followed the leading of His spirit. If I hadn't, there is no way I would be able to share the following revelation with you. What God showed me during this time were so revelatory, powerful, and transformative. So much so, that my daughter and I still look forward to this time.

I found an online Jewish synagogue to stream every Friday evening. Learning the songs, prayers, teachings, and spirit of community changed my life. It opened up scripture to another level in my life. It also allowed me to understand God even more as, "Lord of Economic Kingdoms."

There are two concepts in particular that stand out:

- God as source and supply.
- Sabbath blessing.

There is so much I want to share, and I get excited because God is so brilliant! He hides the deepest concepts in the simplest things. Let's start with a few foundational basics.

God as Source And Supply

"In the beginning, God created the heavens and the earth" (Genesis 1:1). We all know the creation story found in Genesis. On the first day, God said, "Let there be light." Light comes forth. He follows up with each new day by creating another masterpiece.

God is an artist. For almost a week straight, he creates. He saves his most beautiful creation for the sixth day. By the time man arrives on the scene, he has everything he needs, "except woman." God realizes man can't appreciate all he has without having someone to share it with.

God then takes action, bringing woman out of man. Adam and Eve are the perfect power team. God now has two people to enjoy what he has created. Celebrate the goodness of God, and follow in His footsteps by duplicating what He's done.

He tells man and woman together"

- Be fruitful: In other words, "Create."
- Multiply: He did this when he multiplied Adam with Even.
- Replenish and subdue: Restore or restock when needed.
- Have dominion: Reign over everything I've created for you and given you.

This is a duplicatable pattern He set in place for Adam and Eve. It is established for generations to come. The nation of Israel seized this opportunity and maximized this pattern. They made a conscious decision to honor and celebrate the Sabbath.

By the time man arrived on earth's scene, he had everything he needed to thrive. He had the tools, the blessing, and the authority to create, rule, and reign in God's place. Here's the power of the sabbath:

By the time the seventh day arrives, all man has to do is rest. God wants him to celebrate what He has given and wants to receive honor.

This is so powerful. I am going to write an entire book on what God revealed. Adam does not want for anything. He has everything he needs. He has the total supply of heaven and earth. God created everything Adam needed to walk in economic dominion and blessing. God establishes up front that He is man's source!

The Jewish community gets this. They actually see the world through the eyes of creation. They approach family, work, and life with this concept. They approach their week ahead programmed with this mindset. They have six days to create and produce whatever will feed their family now and in the future.

On the seventh day, they pause to recognize the source of all living. They celebrate and bless God's creation. If you grasp this concept, it will be life changing. God creates something with each new day. When he creates anything that is fruitful, he sees that it is good. He blesses it knowing it is able to bring forth and produce more.

The nation of Israel recreates this concept. After working six days, creating something in each and recognizing it is good, they rest on the final day. They bless all they have and offer it back to the Lord to yield more.

During my time observing the Sabbath, my income doubled. I changed tax brackets. I received clients in leading industries with zero marketing. I also created an unbreakable bond with my daughter at the same time. We had time to share our faith together and strengthen our relationship with the Lord.

There is so much more I could say. If you can glean from this, you will start seeing God show out in your life as the Lord of Economic Kingdoms. You will learn how He creates kingdoms and establishes them. You will know how to dominate any industry and system. You will learn that when you keep God first, He's the exponential growth factor.

As I wrote this book, the Holy Spirit woke me up to remind me to touch on two very important principles. They're embedded in the Sabbath blessing.

Sabbath Blessing

While honoring the sabbath, I learned about the Friday night blessing. A person starts the celebration and speaks the blessing. Even as I type I get so excited about it. There is so much to the revelation. I will go into this on a deeper level in future books. Understanding this, is critical to the body of Christ.

For now, let's recite the blessing for those who may be unfamiliar. We won't cover all the blessings right now. For our purposes, I will highlight the blessing right before the sabbath meal.

It consists of blessing the wine and bread:

Blessing of wine (Kiddush)

And there was evening and there was morning, the sixth day.

The heaven and the earth were finished, and all their array. On the seventh day God finished the work that God was doing, and God ceased on the seventh day from all the work that God had done. And God blessed the seventh day and declared it holy, because in it God ceased from all the work of creation that God had done.

Blessed are You, Adonai our God, Sovereign of all, Creator of the fruit of the vine.

Blessed are You, Adonai our God, Sovereign of all, who finding favor with us, sanctified us with *mitzvot*. In love and favor, you made the holy Shabbat our heritage as a reminder of the work of Creation. As first among our sacred days, it recalls the Exodus from Egypt. You chose us and set us apart from the people. In love and favor You have given us Your holy Shabbat as an inheritance. Blessed are You, Adonai, who sanctifies Shabbat.

Washing of Hands

Blessed are You, Lord our God, King of the universe, who has sanctified us with Your commandments, and command us concerning the washing of the hands.

Blessing of Bread (Hamotzi)

Blessed are You, Lord our God, King of the universe, who has brought forth bread from the earth.

This is so significant because it speaks to two things: The Bread and the Body of the Lord Jesus Christ. I cannot go into depth in this writing. I will say for the purposes of this book that when the Body of Christ really understands the power of taking the Lord's communion, it will revolutionize the church. I will share more in future books.

God provides everything we need in him. Let's look at the following scriptures to go deeper:

Matthew 26:26-29 KJV

26 "And as they were eating, Jesus took bread, and blessed it, and brake it, and gave it to the disciples, and said, Take, eat; this is my body.

27 And he took the cup, and gave thanks, and gave it to them, saying, Drink ye all of it;

28 For this is my blood of the new testament, which is shed for many for the remission of sins.

29 But I say unto you, I will not drink henceforth of this fruit of the vine, until that day when I drink it new with you in my Father's kingdom."

In this passage, Jesus was taking communion with his disciples. What I am about to say is very important if you have never studied or understood Jewish culture. Jesus was honoring the sabbath. This was not a random act that did not have historical significance.

I am not sure if this was lost in translation or deliberately reversed, because in Jewish culture they read from left to right. I find it interesting that throughout the bible it always references Jesus taking the bread first and afterward drinking wine. When observing the sabbath, the wine is always blessed first, then hands are washed. Finally, the bread is blessed, broken, and distributed.

God does these in type shadows and patterns. So, let's look at it. Jesus goes to the cross (the bread). He has been sanctified and set apart for the Father's purposes (the cleansing or washing). Finally, after he is crucified and risen again, we see in Acts the Holy Spirit being poured out to the believers (the wine, spirit, or flow of God).

Jesus confirms what I am sharing throughout scripture:

St. John 6:50-58 KJV

50 "This is the bread which cometh down from heaven, that a man may eat thereof, and not die.

51 I am the living bread which came down from heaven: if any man eat of this bread, he shall live for ever: and the bread that I will give is my flesh, which I will give for the life of the world."

52 The Jews therefore strove among themselves, saying, How can this man give us [his] flesh to eat?

53 Then Jesus said unto them, Verily, verily, I say unto you, Except ye eat the flesh of the Son of man, and drink his blood, ye have no life in you.

54 Whoso eateth my flesh, and drinketh my blood, hath eternal life; and I will raise him up at the last day.

55 For my flesh is meat indeed, and my blood is drink indeed.

56 He that eateth my flesh, and drinketh my blood, dwelleth in me, and I in him.

57 As the living Father hath sent me, and I live by the Father: so he that eateth me, even he shall live by me.

58 This is that bread which came down from heaven: not as your fathers did eat manna, and are dead: he that eateth of this bread shall live forever."

Breaking the Bread

Do you know that in Jewish culture, during the blessing of bread, Mizmor leDavid is read? This is Psalms 23. Here is another instance where translation gets lost. In the King James version the first verse reads, "The Lord is my shepherd, I shall not want." In the Hebrew translation it reads, "The Lord is my shepherd, I lack nothing."

It seems so simple. This tiny change makes a dramatic difference from an optic perspective.

Want means: "have a desire to possess or do (something); wish for." So, with this in mind, it would read, The Lord is my shepherd, I shall not have a desire to possess or do (something); wish for. God forbid!

God tells us He wishes above all things that we would prosper (3 John 1-2. He says our soul would prosper and we would be in good health. It's His pleasure to prosper us. Let's look at it through the Hebrew text when we change the wording.

Lack means: "the state of being without or not having enough of something" (Dictionary.com). Let's review it now. "The Lord is my shepherd, I shall not be in a state of being without or not having enough of something."

Words matter. In other cultures, literal definitions mean everything!

As an African American woman growing up in America, there is a mindset that want is ok. There is a mindset that some will have more than enough, and others will be in want. Not so in the Kingdom of God. Say it with me now:

"The Lord is my shepherd, I lack nothing!" Selah

Do you see how it changes everything! Reciting the sabbath blessing is so prophetic. It's an act of declaration and creation for the coming week. Bread represents provision. During certain feasts, Jews will double the amount of bread on the table. This is prophetic. It speaks of what's ahead.

In Matthew 26, Jesus points out that the bread is "His body" which is broken for you. As I shared earlier, God is a solutionist. He solves problems before they exist. Let's look at the life of Jesus. His ministry demonstrated the provision of God. It reflected the miraculous overflow and multiplication of the Father. It confirmed his Sonship in the Kingdom as a testament to God's provision for His children.

Christ tells us as "often as we eat this bread and drink this cup, we do show the Lord's death until he comes" (1 Corinthians 11:26). He instructs us to "Do this in remembrance of me."

The Sabbath is a time of celebration. It captures significant family or community moments. It is a time to study the Torah. It reverences the word of God. It is a time of communion. It strengthens relationships and faith.

When the community comes together on the Sabbath, it is to recount the goodness of God. It is to testify and talk about historical deliverances. It is to recall and retell how God delivered them from their enemies and brought them out of Egypt. It celebrates God's provision as they wandered the wilderness. It speaks of the victory they walked into—possessing the promised land.

During the last supper, Jesus reminds his disciples of one thing. I provided for you when we went to the nations preaching the gospel. In my absence, I will do the same.

He speaks as a prophet to remind the Apostles not to forget. I can hear him in my mind saying, "Don't forget. Don't forget everything you've learned. Don't forget what your eyes have seen. Remember how I walked in flesh with you revealed as a Son. The Father always provides for the son. Don't forget!"

The Father's house has everything you need. There is no lack in it. I find it interesting that even in the secular world, people refer to money as bread. You have to mix and bake bread. It has to rise. It has to expand and grow. You start with basic ingredients and then it rises. It becomes enough to feed an entire family.

Jesus is the bread or provision of life. He gives us identity. He gives salvation. He gives healing. He gives deliverance. He gives eternal life. Because of his life, we have access to his promises and everything we need.

Next, is the blessing on the wine. The wine represents fruitfulness, joy, and replenishment. Wine also represents the work of calvary which gave us the Holy Spirit, the blood of Jesus Christ, and his flow. His Spirit travels free, unbound without limits:

St. John 3:8 KJV

8 "The wind bloweth where it listeth, and thou hearest the sound thereof, but canst not tell whence it cometh, and whither it goeth: so is every one that is born of the Spirit."

Another text says it this way:

Ephesians 1:7 KJV

7 "In whom we have redemption through his blood, the forgiveness of sins, according to the riches of his grace;"

Here's what's critical to remember. When God reveals himself as Lord of Economic Kingdoms, he will work in a flow. He will use His spirit and His body to accomplish what He desires. God uses His body, or people, but there must be unity and a flow.

During Sabbath when they bless the wine and partake in the flow, they speak to being fruitful and the bounty of God. They are declaring replenishment, joyfulness, healing, relationships and more. It's imperative in order to see God's glory manifested in our lives, that we begin to bless people.

I spoke earlier about "hidden treasures in earthen vessels." This is a concept God has dealt with me about for a long time. There are certain levels of flow you can't access if you do not bless God's people.

God distributes wealth according to need. He puts wealth in the hands of those who steward it best. In this hour, He's calling forth those who will reach the less fortunate. He needs those will care for the overlooked and abandoned.

Earlier, I pointed out a text in the book of James (Jesus' younger brother). In chapter 2, verses 14-19 the writer ties your level of faith to what you actually do. It's interesting. He also talks about providing for the poor and destitute as a measure.

How can you expect anyone to believe in a God who consistently overlooks their needs when he is the Father of "ALL" living? This is a misrepresentation of who He is. God says that His ears are not deaf, and His eyes are not too heavy. His arms are not too short to save.

Here's the issue. God's body has become comfortable sitting in church Sunday after Sunday without action. His eyes, ears, and arms (His church) have not been taking steps toward what they say they believe.

This morning as clear as day, I awoke from my sleep hearing the "Footsteps of the Lord." His feet are returning to their place. They are reigning on the throne. Feet move the entire body.

When the woman prepared Jesus for the cross, she worshipped at his feet. This was an act of humility. It's time that humility return to the Body of Christ. When it does, the cup of blessing is going to pour out like never before. Then we will then see the wealth and Lord of Economic Kingdoms show up and show out.

This requires new levels of faith. It requires separation from the world's belief system and way of doing business. Moses said to Pharaoh, "Let my people go." The reason Pharaoh had to let them go was so Israel could go and worship God.

Return to your true place of authenticity, humility, and worship. Then the Lord of Economic Kingdoms will begin to dominate, rule, and govern your affairs and life.

What are you waiting for?

Take some time right now to stop and worship. Think about all the goodness of the Lord. Remember how He brought you out time and time again. Do you remember how you felt when you first believed?

Celebrate what He has done and is doing in you. Celebrate what He is doing in your family.

You are a hidden treasure collected by God for His eternal purposes and glory. God chose you before the foundation of the world. Jesus Christ has a seat for you at the table. He went away to prepare it and has reserved a special room for you in his Father's house.

In the Father's house there are many mansions (John 14:2). Come rest. Come lay down. It is time for refreshing. Break bread with him. Drink of his cup. He wants to show how much He cares. Let Him show you how He's provided.

God wants to reveal Himself as Lord of Economic Kingdoms in your heart and life. He wants you to taste of his Spirit. It's time to partake of His eternal flow!

Get in the Glory Flow

God wants to release large weights and spectacular dimensions of His glory. It will be like never seen before. Think about it—the magnitude of God's glory!

King Solomon was the wealthiest King to exist. His kingdom was so majestic that Queen Sheba (from a faraway country) came to see it. The glory of his kingdom was so splendid that she wanted to glean from his wisdom and take it all.

Can you imagine how the world would marvel if the church of today became the church found in the Book of Acts? Can you imagine what the church would like if the people had "All in common" being on unity in one accord? This is the glory flow.

In God's dominion and flow, there is a continued release of resources. Visions manifest. Households receive blessings to bring forth even more. It produces fruitfulness, replenishment, and overflow. It's where you reap the 100-fold increase, and a double portion unfolds.

It is an unconventional and uncommon way to live. Most people won't stretch and cannot stretch to this level. It requires new dimensions of faith. You have to leave dependency on the status quo. You have to stop the hustle and bustle long enough to acknowledge God in everything.

When everyone else is hanging out having fun, those in the glory flow are at home lighting a candle of praise. They show gratitude for what is already given. They release their faith about promises to come. They speak to family and loved ones about God's goodness. They study scripture and make sure future generations do not forget what God has done.

My story about getting to know the Lord of Economic Kingdoms started over 20 years ago. At the time, I didn't realize God was releasing wealth into my hands. I thought the reason God revealed this to me in prayer was for others. This was only true in part.

I didn't recognize my own identity in Christ. I didn't comprehend what God was showing me. I sat on this revelation and completely forgot about it until 2018, experiencing "Spiritual Amnesia." The enemy attempted his best to throw so much at me and cause distraction.

Now, God has revealed this revelation is much bigger than me. So many are like I was, waiting for affirmation outside to follow the leading of the voice within. God's spirit is still talking, but many are missing out on the flow.

Stop waiting for your local pastor, a prophet, or your best friend. No one else can affirm the gift of God in you. God has distributed gifts which produce the wealth of God according to every man's faith:

Ephesians 4:7-8 KJV

7 "But unto every one of us is given grace according to the measure of the gift of Christ.

8 Wherefore he saith, When he ascended up on high, he led captivity captive, and gave gifts unto men."

Start seeking God today about the reason He put you here on this earth. Ask diligently what He has called you to do:

Matthew 6:33 KJV

33 "But seek ye first the kingdom of God, and his righteousness; and all these things shall be added unto you

This scripture sounds so cliché, but it is 100% true. When you put God and His people first, you can't help but walk in the "blessing that maketh rich and he adds no sorrow to it" (Proverbs 10:22). Stop waiting on the sidelines.

No longer does the Lord of Economic Kingdoms desire for us to wait on someone else. It is no one else's responsibility to identify the gifts or wealth you carry inside. We can no longer depend on systems that exclude God from the equation. He does not want us to worry about the cares of this life, or how we will make it and get by.

Matthew 6:19-34 KJV

19 "Lay not up for yourselves treasures upon earth, where moth and rust doth corrupt, and where thieves break through and steal:

20 But lay up for yourselves treasures in heaven, where neither moth nor rust doth corrupt, and where thieves do not break through nor steal:

21 For where your treasure is, there will your heart be also.

22 The light of the body is the eye: if therefore thine eye be single, thy whole body shall be full of light.

23 But if thine eye be evil, thy whole body shall be full of darkness. If therefore the light that is in thee be darkness, how great is that darkness!

24 No man can serve two masters: for either he will hate the one, and love the other; or else he will hold to the one, and despise the other. Ye cannot serve God and mammon.

25 Therefore I say unto you, Take no thought for your life, what ye shall eat, or what ye shall drink; nor yet for your body, what ye shall put on. Is not the life more than meat, and the body than raiment?

26 Behold the fowls of the air: for they sow not, neither do they reap, nor gather into barns; yet your heavenly Father feedeth them. Are ye not much better than they?

27 Which of you by taking thought can add one cubit unto his stature?

28 And why take ye thought for raiment? Consider the lilies of the field, how they grow; they toil not, neither do they spin:

29 And yet I say unto you, That even Solomon in all his glory was not arrayed like one of these.

30 Wherefore, if God so clothe the grass of the field, which to day is, and tomorrow is cast into the oven, shall he not much more clothe you, O ye of little faith?

31 Therefore take no thought, saying, What shall we eat? or, What shall we drink? or, Wherewithal shall we be clothed?

32 (For after all these things do the Gentiles seek:) for your heavenly Father knoweth that ye have need of all these things.

33 But seek ye first the kingdom of God, and his righteousness; and all these things shall be added unto you.

34 Take therefore no thought for the morrow: for the morrow shall take thought for the things of itself. Sufficient unto the day is the evil thereof."

Birds and flowers are highlighted in the passage above. God creates each to fulfill His purposes. As the scripture demonstrates, birds and flowers do not worry about how God will provide. They do not show concern for anything other than serving their purpose.

It insults God when we minimize God's provision. As our Heavenly Father, He understands our needs. He reminds us the very hairs of our head are all numbered (Luke 12:7). Not trusting him to meet our needs is a reflection of where our faith lies. It stops the flow of blessings and relationships in our lives.

Staying in the flow requires internal reflection and transparency. Think about the following questions:

- What treasures do you have in your life?
- Where do your treasures lie?
- Who or what is your faith in?
- Who or what have you allowed to become your source?
- Who or what do you turn to when you have a need?
- How much time do you stop to thank God for all He's done?
- What are your natural born gifts and talents?
- What are your God-given abilities?
- What are you called in this earth to do?
- What are you creating every day to bless others?

Recognize who and whose you are. Decide to take your rightful place as a joint heir with Christ. Choose to access all the benefits and provision God has store in for you. Your true inheritance is waiting. Are you ready to claim it?

Claiming Your Inheritance

Let's discuss the story of a little shepherd boy. David fought many battles. Later, he became king. Before him, King Saul, reigned. Saul was so, tall and handsome. The people chose Saul. King David, on the other hand, was chosen by God because he was a man after God's heart (Acts 13:22).

David found favor in God's sight and this favor allowed him to rule for generations to come. King David fought his way to the throne. He saw a lot of bloodshed and was a man of war. However, David sinned against God when he killed Uriah to cover his sin of adultery with the man's wife (2 Samuel 11).

The woman, Bathsheba, became pregnant with King David's child. David had Uriah murdered in battle. The child dies. David mourns. David marries Bathsheba and she gets pregnant again. The child, Solomon, is conceived.

Solomon grows to be the next King of Israel. In 1 Kings 3:12, God pronounces wisdom on Solomon and the nation experiences the most peace it's ever had in its history.

1 Kings 3:12

12 "I have given you a wise and understanding heart, so that there has not been anyone like you before you, nor shall any like you arise after you."
This story highlights:

- King David as a man of war. He takes down giants and defeats nations.
- King David increases and expands Israel's territory, resources, wealth and dominion.
- King David's history is not without blemish. He has a son born through an imperfect union.
- As King David grows old, he is no longer able to reign. He makes Solomon King.

- King Solomon inherits the throne. He is given authority and rule over the entire kingdom. He doesn't have to fight any wars at all.
- King Solomon has full access to the nation's provision and providence to use at his discretion.
- King Solomon increases and expands Israel's territory, resources, wealth, and dominion.

This story is the perfect pattern of what took place when Jesus went to Calvary. He fought many battles so we could live through victory and peace. He took on Satan demonstrating the Kingdom of God everywhere he went.

After Christ died, he rose with all power in his hands (Matthew 28:18). He ascended to the throne and is seated at the right hand of God (Colossians 3:1). He receives all power in heaven and earth (1 Chronicles 29:11). Through Him, we now have access to the Father (Ephesians 2:18). We are joint heirs with Christ (Romans 8:17) and have inherited the Kingdom of God.

Revelation 5:9-12 KJV

9 "And they sung a new song, saying, Thou art worthy to take the book, and to open the seals thereof: for thou wast slain, and hast redeemed us to God by thy blood out of every kindred, and tongue, and people, and nation;

10 And hast made us unto our God kings and priests: and we shall reign on the earth.

11 And I beheld, and I heard the voice of many angels round about the throne and the beasts and the elders: and the number of them was ten thousand times ten thousand, and thousands of thousands;

12 Saying with a loud voice, Worthy is the Lamb that was slain to receive power, and riches, and wisdom, and strength, and honour, and glory, and blessing."

This passage assures us:

- Jesus Christ is slain for the sins of the world.

- We are kings and priests.
- We have authority to reign "on earth".
- Our inheritance package comes with power, riches, wisdom, strength, honour, glory, and blessing.

Are you ready to receive your inheritance?
Many in the Body of Christ do not know who they are. They lack identity. For those who grow up in two parent households with a strong family background, this may not be the case. If you're like me, you grew up without your father in the home. You may not know what it is like to have a protector and provider as a role model.

Accessing the fullness of your Heavenly Father is possible. The key is being able to identify what He's given. God's eternal weight of glory can be inconceivable at times. It takes the word of God and the Holy Spirit to reveal it to you.

Many find it hard to believe for provision. Their faith or belief systems have not matured to this place. Christ has reigned for thousands of years, yet it is hard for many to accept the totality of what that looks like and means. They relate to Jesus, but have yet to find their identity in him.

Provision and identity tie together. A person can only claim their inheritance when they claim their seat in heavenly places. Like your identity, your wealth is also hidden in Christ Jesus too. To access it, your faith has to rise. Your language has to change.

Your language has to change!

- Your language has to change about who you are.
- Your language has to change concerning what you have.
- Your language has to change regarding what you can do.

Jesus is the same yesterday, today and forever more (Hebrews 13:8). He establishes patterns. So in heaven, so it is in the earth. In the Old Testament, God gave Moses the blueprint to build the tabernacle. It resembled the heavenly tabernacle already established in heaven.

When Jesus ascended to take His rightful place next to the Father (Mark 16:19), He also established a pattern. This pattern of eternal rule established in heaven was also given to those who believe. We have access to his power. We have access to his honor. We have access to his riches. We have access to his glory.

So many relate to Jesus as savior, healer, shepherd, deliverer, and teacher. Yet, unless a person understands him as Lord of Economic Kingdoms, they will miss it. Jesus performed so many miracles which demonstrated economic empowerment, money, or wealth in some way:

- Jesus' first miracle he turns water to wine. Wine represented health, happiness, and prosperity.
- Jesus multiplies five loaves and two fish to feed 5,000.
- Jesus increases Simon Peter and the disciples net of fish.
- Jesus instructs Peter to catch a fish. The fish has a coin in its mouth to pay Jesus and Peter's tax.
- Wine and fish were industries of trade.
- Jesus brings salvation to the tax collector's house.

Jesus showed up as Lord of Economic Kingdoms. The fact that he was called "King of the Jews" (Matthew 27:37) while here on earth is remarkable in itself. He preached to the poor and healed the sick everywhere he went. He dominated over everything around him.

St. John 14:12 KJV

12 "Verily, verily, I say unto you, He that believeth on me, the works that I do shall he do also; and greater works than these shall he do; because I go unto my Father."
So many believers pray for signs, miracles, and wonders. You can believe God to show out in your life as Lord of Economic Kingdoms, too.

I love it when He reminds me of the day I heard the phrase ringing in my ear. It was with such power and authority. It kept reverberating over and over. The phrase has so much significance because a kingdom is defined as: "A country, state, or territory ruled by a king or queen" (Dictionary.com).

He did not say "Economic kingdom," but rather "Kingdoms," which is plural. This is profound. It is where we get into systematic wealth structures and economic territories. Not only is He Lord of Economic Kingdoms, but He reigns over laws and principles that govern them. Even those very laws that rule and dominate economic kingdoms have to bow to Him!

Will You Believe?

Mark 9:23 KJV

23 "Jesus said unto him, If thou canst believe, all things are possible to him that believeth."
Jesus came through the lineage of King David to die for the sins of the world. He came so we can have access to all of his kingdom and promises. We reign with him in eternity. We have full access to all the benefits of our Heavenly Father's kingdom. We have His love, provision, and providence. He has left our divine inheritance and estate.

To claim an estate or inheritance, a person must be listed in the last will and testament. Christ, the testator, has written us into His last will and testament through the Word of God. Our faith and salvation give us the title deed. It is waiting for us to possess it. Once possessed, it must be enforced.

Enforcing this wealth strategy requires changing your language. You must change what you say and how you respond. This strategy intercepts and confuses the communication system of the enemy.

If your faith has not risen to this level, invoke your heavenly language to build it. Speaking in tongues as the Spirit gives utterance will confound your enemy. This may seem so simple and foolish, however:

I Corinthians 1:27 KJV

27 "But God hath chosen the foolish things of the world to confound the wise; and God hath chosen the weak things of the world to confound the things which are mighty;

28 And base things of the world, and things which are despised, hath God chosen, yea, and things which are not, to bring to nought things that are:

29 That no flesh should glory in his presence."

- What are you telling yourself about your current financial situation?
- What are you believing God for?
- What promises do you still need to claim?
- What have you been finding your identity in?
- What language do you need to change?

Romans 10:8 KJV

8 "But what saith it? The word is nigh thee, even in thy mouth, and in thy heart: that is, the word of faith, which we preach."

Romans 4:17 KJV

17 "(As it is written, I have made thee a father of many nations,) before him whom he believed, even God, who quickeneth the dead, and calleth those things which be not as though they were."

Joel 3:10 KJV

10 "Beat your plowshares into swords and your pruninghooks into spears: let the weak say, I am strong."

Now is the time to, "Let the weak say I am strong. Let the poor say I am rich" (Joel 3:10). Rise up to possess the kingdom because the "Kingdom of God is at hand!"

Thy Kingdom Come

This revelation given to me by the Holy Spirit is much bigger than a prosperity message. It is about the will of God on earth as it is in heaven. It is about the Kingdom of the living God manifesting on earth in all its glory. A dying world needs to know the living God.

The church must begin to establish economic wealth and structures in the earth. These will outperform human structures and systems. Up until now, there have not been alternatives to wicked solutions to fill the need.

Think about it. The industry of human trafficking is at an all-time high. Child pornography and sexual deviation is out of control. The drug industry is rampant. Suicide among youth is higher than it's ever been.

The entertainment industry has no filter. Social media lacks discretion. Divorce has become the standard. Hate-filled conversation rules the media. These kingdoms or systems can no longer stay in place. The government or rule of divine law and order must return.

Kingdom leaders, wealth generators, and generational visionaries are being raised up. They will establish economic systems. They will lead with compassion, love, provision, providence, happiness, and prosperity. God wants to unveil His glory. This transformation coming to the Body of Christ is going to be mind blowing. It will bring adoration and glory to God.

Globally, the culture of the world will shift. We will see a manifestation of the "Kingdoms of this world become the Kingdoms of our God" (Revelation 11:15).

Revelation 11:15 KJV

15 "And the seventh angel sounded; and there were great voices in heaven, saying, The kingdoms of this world are become the kingdoms of our Lord, and of his Christ; and he shall reign for ever and ever."

Wars will cease. Nations will heal. Creation will sing. God will be glorified. Then everyone everywhere on one accord will join to say:

Matthew 6:9-13 KJV

9 "After this manner therefore pray ye: Our Father which art in heaven, Hallowed be thy name.

10 Thy kingdom come, Thy will be done in earth, as it is in heaven.

11 Give us this day our daily bread.

12 And forgive us our debts, as we forgive our debtors.

13 And lead us not into temptation, but deliver us from evil: For thine is the kingdom, and the power, and the glory, for ever. Amen."

We, the Body of Christ can begin to access all fullness of His kingdom, power, and glory. We can experience new dimensions of His provision. We can get to know him as Lord of Economic Kingdoms, where He reigns and rules over all.

Author's Notes

Every year I have the privilege to speak to new audiences around the world to ignite hope and transformation. There is nothing more satisfying than seeing new relationships form, dead dreams come alive, and untapped potential turn to power.

I remember the first time I spoke in front of an audience. I was a 14-year-old Texan with a message for the world. I was born to speak and teach. I love connecting with audiences to share real-world experiences, proven principles, and breakthrough strategies.

I've spent decades inspiring and investing in people. I've challenged the status quo and provoked change with powerful messages that go against conventional wisdom. Whether a Fortune 500 company, educational institution, or nonprofit, my passion is to help others break out-of-the-box to see new possibilities and experience exponential growth.

Thank you for reading this book! When I wrote the book I was in a time of deep reflection. At that time, I realized I was looking in others for what I'd hope to find within. I pray you are inspired to take action and run quickly into the open arms of your Heavenly Father. He's always there to pick us up when we need Him most.

Who Is Lonna Hardin

Lonna Hardin is a woman of faith who leads with love, light, and integrity. Through music, the multi-gifted creative educates, speaks, and sings to the souls that are thirsty for God's love and grace, just as she is.

The ambitious single mother from the midwest has experienced many tests and trials, only equipping her to become strengthened in her faith and gracefully transformed into God's image.

Lonna is an authentic Christian leader who honors her Lord and savior and has cultivated many businesses and organizations that embody the visions God has blessed her with to be a blessing to others.

In addition to being an author and inspiration to others, Lonna is a Gospel radio-hit making recording artist who's smooth, sultry voice has been featured on the top 150 U.S. gospel stations around the world. She also received worldwide recognition as #17 on the International Top 30 Artist list.

Now, Lonna sings, writes, and speaks, with audiences around the world. She's also a voice to add light to issues that impact the voiceless and vulnerable.

Lonna is acclaimed author of several books including, 'Voiceprint and the Melody's Song children's book series, as well as a powerful faith-based series. Her books are featured at libraries, bookstores, museums, and and events across the country.

You've seen or heard her inspire on TBN, Black Gospel, Storytelling Companion, and television or radio stations around the world.

Lonna Hardin's high-spirited energy and message of hope is why audiences say they experience the wow factor after hearing Lonna sing or speak at conferences, workshops, seminars, and events. To see Lonna 'Live or book her at your next event, visit lonnahardin.com

Lonna Hardin Enterprises
lonnahardin.com

www.ingramcontent.com/pod-product-compliance
Lightning Source LLC
Chambersburg PA
CBHW051431090426
42737CB00014B/2925